DATE DUE

WESTERN POLICY
AND
THE THIRD WORLD

THOMAS PATRICK MELADY

WESTERN

POLICY
AND THE
THIRD WORLD

General Editor
EDWARD WAKIN

awthorn Books, Inc.   Publishers   New York

3250

To Christina
who has brought us such happiness

PREFACE

In *The Revolution of Color* I recorded my analysis of the rise to power of the Afro-Asian peoples which occurred simultaneously with the end of time and distance. Confrontation is now, for the first time in world history, taking place between men and cultures; white and black, brown, yellow and red, so long separated by vast distances, now live in the same world village. These historic changes have significant political, social and economic implications.

Now that the peoples of color have some power in world affairs for the first time in modern history, what are the precise implications for the West? What was Western policy before these changes? What is that policy now and what should it be?

The mystique of the Third World includes the swift changes taking place in the Negro community of the United States. What is the relationship between the more than 20 million American Negroes and United States policy?

7

WESTERN POLICY AND THE THIRD WORLD is designed as a companion piece to *The Revolution of Color*. Both books have been written for the general public.

Some of the ideas in this book were developed in lectures before audiences in Europe, Africa and the United States. Discussions with these audiences following the lectures frequently have helped me to clarify some of my own thoughts on these matters.

There are friends in Africa, Asia, Europe and in the United States who have assisted me in obtaining data and in formulating some of my own viewpoints. To these friends go my warmest thanks.

I am especially indebted to Mr. Edward Wakin for his careful reading of the first draft to the manuscript and for his editorial recommendations.

My wife Margaret has been a source of inspiration throughout the development of both *The Revolution of Color* and this book. She has participated with me in our conversations with people from all parts of the world, for she, like me, believes that by determining the facts and the implications of the presence in world affairs of the peoples of color we can in a small way help to establish the dialogue that will lead us all who now live in the same world village to greater harmony. Margaret also assisted me with the necessary tasks of proofreading the several drafts.

While friends have assisted me in obtaining data and formulating conclusions, I accept full responsibility for all the information set forth and the judgments that have been made.

THOMAS PATRICK MELADY

1967
New York City

CONTENTS

Appendices

CHAPTER ONE

ARMAGEDDON AND

THE THIRD WORLD

. . . who go abroad to the kings of the whole world, to assemble them for battle on the great day of God the Almighty. And they assembled them at the place which is called in Hebrew Armageddon (REV., xvi, 15, 16)

The continuous chain of battle and cataclysm in the two decades since the end of World War II has dulled reactions everywhere to each new Armageddon. The unheard-of, the unexpected, the "impossible" have become part of the daily diet in the press and in the broadcasting media. In these mercurial and menacing twenty years, science has been overwhelming in its promise and in its threat to the world. Our basic institutions have been caught in a process of change that accelerates with each passing year. The family, the school, the church are being transformed and propelled in directions that are still unpredictable. Government, business and education

11

are racing to keep pace with conditions that change overnight. And in each individual there is the daily struggle to adjust to change.

We are faced with the historic emergence of the majority of the human race in the non-white world—a Third World centered in Asia and Africa; but the significance of this change becomes lost in the compelling distractions of daily journalism, which pours forth crisis in haste. This can obscure the momentous fact that a Third World has become a reality in world affairs. Some starkly simple reminders can help to restore a perspective so easily distorted by the rush of single events that can seem so baffling, so unrelated.

It is necessary to draw up short and underline the magnitude of the worldwide changeover. For centuries—actually from the time of the Romans—world power has been concentrated in the white West. All worldwide power decisions were made in this part of the world, all power was concentrated here. There were many arguments and wars within this power structure. Millions were slaughtered and killed, but the power never left this part of the world. The beginning of the end of this era came in World War II, when the dread Western aberrations of the Nazis and the Fascists were coupled with the expansionist tendencies of the Japanese Empire. United, their forces attacked the democratic West and then the new power factor arising in the Soviet Union, the Communist state. While the combined forces of the democratic West and the Soviet State were victorious, a new element had been injected into the West's internal struggle. The century's first major non-white political power growth, the Japanese Empire, had appeared on the scene to challenge the West.

With the founding of the United Nations in 1945, a familiar Western monopoly seemed firmly entrenched. Even the struggle for power was concentrated on the European continent. The Atlantic Community, led, powered and managed by the United States, confronted the Warsaw Pact power complex dominated by the Soviet Union. Then, on September 21, 1949, a towering Asian element was introduced into the situation with the proclamation of the People's Republic of China by the Chinese People's Political Consultative Conference under Mao Tse-tung. The label *people's* had by then developed a standardized meaning; it meant Communist. This was one Armageddon, a nation of three-quarters of a billion people under the Communist banner. On February 15, 1950, the USSR and the "People's Republic" signed a 300-year treaty of "friendship, alliance and mutual assistance."

Two events traced in the simplicity of geographical statistics dramatize the process that was sweeping the world. The West was no longer overlord in Asia and in Africa—as in India and as in Algeria. These two countries, in particular, symbolized the Third World's emergence out of the Western colonial shadows.

On August 15, 1947, India became independent. A nation of 1.3 million square miles became free of the United Kingdom, a nation of 94,000 square miles. Forty years of struggle had ended for a nation comprising 471 million people.

On July 3, 1962, fifteen years later, Algeria became independent, reflecting the lag in African independence when compared with Asia. But with Algeria, a stubborn stronghold of resistance crumbled; the pace of events in Africa had already become irresistible. Algeria, a country of 900,000 square miles, became independent of France, a country less than one-fourth its size.

By introducing the statistics of comparative size and by citing the rapid timetable of independence, we underline the significant starting point for our discussion. Large masses of people and huge territories suddenly and irrevocably became independent of industrialized nations, which by comparison were small in size and population. This is a fundamental and crucial reality that is too easily obscured in the complications of analysis and the dialectic of ideologies. Power had changed hands from the few to the many.

One other Armageddon will help to make the point that the geopolitical context had changed dramatically. This was the Suez crisis, which symbolized the sinking of gunboat diplomacy and the setting of the sun upon the empire period. Like the ribbon of water it is, the Suez Canal flows from the peak of British and French colonialism to its demise.

The Canal's origins belong entirely to another period. A French corporation under Ferdinand de Lesseps built the Canal and the masterful Disraeli, while Prime Minister of Britain, obtained control of the Canal for his country. In November 1875, Disraeli called an emergency cabinet meeting, cowed his ministers, side-stepped his Parliament and borrowed the money (4 million pounds) from the House of Rothschild.

It was the charismatic era of the grand tactic, the individual flourish and the single-minded power of the West. That day seems so far away when Disraeli's secretary rushed into the office of Lionel Rothschild and asked for the money to buy the Canal. Rothschild asked what was the security for the loan.

"The British government," replied the courier.

"You shall have it," answered Rothschild.

Eighty-one years later, after Egyptian President Gamal Abdel Nasser nationalized the Suez Canal on July 26, 1956, a nuclear war threatened to explode upon the world. The 103 miles of canal connecting the Mediterranean and the Red Sea, the transportation lifeline which is as narrow as 200 feet in some of its stretches, sits with Africa on one bank and Asia on the other. It is the most likely of fulcrums on which to balance the might of East and West and the most sensitive of the tendons connecting the non-white worlds of Asia and Africa.

When Britain and France followed Israel's October 29, 1956, invasion of Egypt by occupying Port Said at the Mediterranean end of the Canal, the world trembled on the edge of war. As British and French troops moved southward, occupying the Canal, both the United States and Russia pressured the invaders to withdraw. In retrospect, the United States-Russian opposition to the action of Britain and France epitomized one of the many strange combinations that have become characteristic of the fluctuations of cold war diplomacy. The Russians then rattled their rockets, which forced the United States to counter with a threat of retaliation if Russia attacked French and British cities—although the United States still opposed British-French action in Suez.

When the United Nations emergency forces took over the situation on December 22 and the invasion forces withdrew, more than an ill-fated adventure had failed. For the colonial powers an entire pattern of power—the ability to impose their way by force as well as financing—had gone into rapid decline. Not that residual attempts to hold on have stopped— witness Portugal. But with Suez, the world watched the end of colonial pre-eminence. All that was left was worldwide withdrawal, sooner or later.

All these forces of change had been set loose by World War II and as soon as the war ended, they swept through Asia and Africa. First it was in the Far East, where Indonesia, Burma, India and Pakistan established the pattern of independence. Then it was extended to the Near and Middle East and to North Africa, where Libya was born with United Nations approval in 1949.

In 1957, the first black nation, Ghana, achieved independence and the force of change developed momentum. Within a few years West, Central and East Africa—once subservient dominions of the West—became sovereign and independent states. The Third World of the Afro-Asian peoples had risen to its feet with a dramatic suddenness that startled the old empires.

The appearance of a Third World in international affairs brought with it other reactions and changes. It bolstered the non-white peoples residing in the West in throwing off second-class status. They drew strength and encouragement from the fact that non-white peoples in Africa and Asia had achieved the dignity of independence. There is clearly an interlocking relationship between the more than twenty million American Negroes and the Negro peoples living in Africa and the Caribbean. The extent and nature of this relationship may be discussed and disputed, but the relationship exists.

Although the power structure has changed and the world map now consists of three power groupings—the West, the Sino-Soviet bloc, and the Third World—the full impact of the power changes has not yet been felt in the socio-economic and cultural areas. When this happens in the coming years, the changes may be even more significant than the worldwide political changes.

A related phenomenon in the rise to power of the Afro-Asian peoples has been the acceleration of social conscious-ness among Christian forces. The visit of Pope Paul VI to the United Nations in 1965 was a clear affirmation of the deter-mination of the Catholic Church to identify itself with the aspirations of the peoples of color who constitute the bulk of the deprived two-thirds of the world's population. They have the lowest per capita income, the shortest life span, the most depressed life situation. They are afflicted by the triple curse of poverty, illiteracy and disease. The Christian forces, both Catholic and Protestant, have increasingly stressed the moral responsibility of the affluent, developed nations, mostly in the West, to assist the deprived two-thirds of the world's population. Within a few short years, the forces of the Afro-Asian peoples have found common ground with Christian movements in world affairs. In this regard, the Encyclical letter "On the Development of Peoples" by Pope Paul VI is one of the most comprehensive documents ever issued on the needs of the emerging nations. It is the Magna Carta of the Third World.

The change in world politics which has produced three groupings of power has been followed by a staggering revolution in distance. The Afro-Asian peoples—formerly weeks away from the white West—are now the next-door neighbors of citizens living in London and New York. Modern communication makes it possible for millions of people to know what happens within a few hours in the remotest parts of the world. As the world grows smaller and smaller, all peoples become next-door neighbors, residents of a single global village.

Meanwhile, responsible men everywhere are staggered by the horrors of potential nuclear warfare, and the Third World watches with repugnance the balance of nuclear terror in the world. It is only natural that the deprived peoples should respond with disgust to large sums spent for world destruction while most of the human race struggles to reach a minimum level of human dignity. Pope Paul's pacifist United Nations visit in 1965 won a warm response from the Afro-Asian peoples.

It is evident that there have been significant changes in world affairs. Old empires have faded and some have fallen. New nations and power groupings have arisen. New alliances between religious forces and power groupings have been forged. In many ways a new pluralism, both politically and theologically, is appearing on the world scene. As mankind moves toward the year 2000, the significant political changes that have occurred since the end of World War II will have their momentous effect on worldwide customs and traditions. The resulting changes in the affairs of men will have more significance than mere changes on the map of the world.

For the West and its policies in the Afro-Asian world, the challenge is inescapable. New realities call for appropriate responses and these responses must be fashioned out of a realistic and informed perspective. The West must be guided by realism, yes, but it also has a tradition of humanism, of freedom, of idealism to uphold. Out of both—realism and idealism—the white, Christian and affluent West must evolve a policy for the majority of the world which is not white, not Christian and not wealthy.

CHAPTER TWO

PROBLEMS OF
MULTIPLICATION AND
DIVISION

New nations multiply. New divisions appear. New alignments emerge from conference and conclave. Commitments that were made in the twilight of empire are violated in the dawn of Afro-Asian emergence. Out of these problems of multiplication and division, a familiar pattern has resulted: all the world is divided into three parts. It is taken for granted that in the coming decades there will be the West, the East and those countries comprising a Third World of Afro-Asian nations (including those "neutral" in favor of the West and those "neutral" in favor of the East).

However, this world view can be misleading if it is seen through the perspective of the major powers as a choice between East and West. The predominant policy of the Third World arises from a legitimately obsessive concern with victory

19

over poverty, illiteracy and disease. That threefold goal governs their often misunderstood actions and policies at home and abroad.

While the conventional three-way division of the world has limitations, it does have shattering impact upon the policies of the Afro-Asian nations. The division begins with the paramount force, represented by the West, which held the imperial sceptre in the modern period and then lost its monopoly position. Its cultural heart is in Western Europe, its main strength in North America and its appendages in South America and Australia. The Sino-Soviet bloc, whose newness is often overlooked when it is evaluated as a counterforce to the West, took its ideology and direction from Soviet Communism and spread westward to the satellite countries before spreading eastward to China. However, what France has done to the unity of the North Atlantic Treaty Organization, Communist China has outdone with the Communist bloc. Just as Europe has developed economic alternatives to the United States in its own prosperity, Communist satellites have been encouraged to seek more independent roles by the relative success of Communist China.

As soon as these standard divisions—which have become part of the journalistic catechism of international affairs—are explored, new complications appear beneath the surface. United States policy coincides, in certain problems, with Russian strategy. France finds Communist China a sometime bedfellow. England finds it necessary to clarify, the United States to reiterate intentions, West Germany demands explanations, de Gaulle waves the banner of French glory. Red China denounces Soviet Russia for playing the American game, Canada sells wheat to Red China, France vetoes British entry into the European Common Market—and so the world of the two great power complexes mounts complication upon tactic and maneuver upon policy. It is a problem of division beneath a surface of unity.

In the Third World of Afro-Asian nations, it is a matter of multiplication—of new nations born yesterday and trying to mature overnight. They have appeared suddenly at the United Nations, each with one vote, many ideals and many problems. The dramatic African emergence began with the admission of Libya to the United Nations in 1955. In 1956 it was Sudan, Morocco and Tunisia; in 1957 Ghana; in 1958 Guinea; in 1960—the "year of Africa"—thirteen members of the French Community along with the Congo (Leopoldville), Nigeria and Somali. Then in 1961, Sierra Leone, Mauritania and Tanganyika were admitted to the United Nations, followed by Rwanda, Burundi, Algeria and Uganda in 1962, and by Malawi and Zambia in 1964. In the fall of 1966, the Afro-Asian representation at the United Nations totaled about one-half the total membership.

In their approach to this Third World of non-aligned and underdeveloped nations, both East and West have tended to impose an either-or demand: either FOR or AGAINST. Only by dint of refusal and resistance have new nations gained full independence in a new sense—independence of a worldwide competition which they did not create.

The Communist bloc is obsessive in seeing the world as its battleground, while the West sees the world as its concern and opposes Communist takeovers. The two blocs confront each other with confidence in their respective causes, and the confidence has produced a startling arithmetic developed by Communist strategists, particularly the following view[1] of the Communist future as foreseen by Soviet expert S. Strumilin:

[1] Quoted by Zbigniew Brzezinski as editor of *Africa and the Communist World* (Stanford, California: Stanford University Press, 1963), pp. 5–6.

We may recall that the growth in the population of the socialist camp attributable to the addition of new members just since 1945, after the World War, reached not less than 830,000,000 persons by 1960, and of these not more than 80,000,000 came from the countries liberated from Hitler's yoke, while about 750,000,000 are from the underdeveloped parts of the world, representing some 36 percent of its population. It can be expected that in the future this irreversible process of the socialist camp's expansion will proceed according to approximately the same rates and volumes.

But let us assume out of caution that not more than 30 percent of the population of neutral countries and not more than 10 percent of those of the imperialist camp take the socialist road during the next twenty years, and then in the first decade—up to 1970— the percentages are only half of these. In this case, the movements of the world's population during the twenty years will appear approximately as in the table below:

WORLD POPULATION (MILLIONS)

Groups of Countries	1960 Total	1960 %	1970 Total	1970 %	1980 Total	1980 %
Socialist	1,050	35	1,597	45	2,295	54
Imperialist	600	20	631	18	660	16
Other	1,350	45	1,318	37	1,248	30

Fortunately, the "irreversible process" is much more wish than reality. More than two-thirds of Africa has become independent without any movement into the Communist camp. In Asia, the tragedy of Korea and Vietnam required armed Communist intervention reminiscent of Soviet actions in creating satellites, but nowhere in the Far East has Communism been an irresistible force carrying all before it. If colonialism has been the known devil to the newly liberated Afro-Asian nations, Communism has been more the unknown devil than the avenging angel. While the new elites in the Afro-Asian countries resent past exploitation and colonial domination, they have not blindly accepted Communism as the road to modernization. While the Afro-Asian elite may regard capitalism as a flawed system unsuited—in pure undiluted form—to their situation, they apply a similarly critical view toward Communism.

Meanwhile, Communist China, the most ruthless participant in Communist operations, has openly undermined the Russians and thereby weakened the Communist solid front by emphasizing racism. The Chinese have become increasingly blunt in aligning themselves with the Afro-Asian peoples against all whites, Russians included. For instance, at the 1962 Afro-Asian Conference in Cairo, one Chinese delegate went so far as to speak of the "importance of us blacks sticking together." The common theme of the Red Chinese to non-whites is that "only we can understand your problems."

At the same time, the Red Chinese lack the military and economic strength to offer massive aid and assistance to underdeveloped nations. They have sought to introduce dramatic assistance and have tended to ignore normal economic safeguards in extending aid. With them, the diplomatic and tactical aims are paramount and some Africans, at least, have discerned what amounts to indifference about the positive results for the recipient country. The Chinese want *in,* and their intentions are as ruthless as their methods. The Chinese offer revolutionary zeal and the traditional tenacity and skill of Chinese abroad; and the many Chinese millionaires in Asian countries testify to the effectiveness of Chinese in the marketplaces of faraway places.

On the diplomatic level, Chinese success can be shown in the growing number of African nations which have recognized Communist China. Bearing in mind that the United Arab Republic was the first African nation to extend recognition (and this was not until 1956), the record has been impressive.

By the end of 1960, Morocco, Sudan, Guinea, Ghana, Mali and Somalia had recognized Red China and by February 1964, they were joined by Tanganyika, Algeria, Uganda, Kenya, Zanzibar (later joined with Tanganyika to form Tanzania), Burundi, Tunisia and Congo (Brazzaville).

In its campaign in Asia and Africa, Communist China has consistently singled out the United States as the single great enemy against a background of "Western, colonial, imperialist enemies." This is an outgrowth of the China problem in which the antagonists were the United States–supported Chiang Kai-shek and the Soviet-supported Mao Tse-tung. In the straits of Formosa, in Korea and in Vietnam, the United States and Red China have stood gun to gun in dangerous and bloody confrontation.

To the Red Chinese the single overriding foreign enemy is the United States, and in this regard there is a significant difference in emphasis between the Russians and the Chinese. While the United States is Russia's most powerful antagonist, Soviet tactics are not as obsessive and not as overwhelmed by the United States as the only enemy. In this context, the Red Chinese have been quick to denounce any sign of accommodation between Russian and United States aims in the Afro-Asian world.

To select a single month—November 1965—propaganda statements from Peking dramatize the Red Chinese use of "pro-United States" charge to strike out at the Russians. On November 10, 1965, *The People's Daily* in Peking published a 30,000-word indictment of the Moscow behavior toward the Vietnam war and accused the Russians of trying to persuade the North Vietnamese to accept "unconditional negotiations" with the United States. On November 16, Pravda and Izvestia counterattacked by accusing Communist China of depicting Soviet support of the North Vietnamese as collusion with

American imperialism. On November 20, the official organ of the East German Communist Party published a long article under the headline "USSR Slanderously Accused by Chinese Newspapers of Making Common Cause with the United States." The article said that the Chinese "again and again" give reasons for Westerners to conclude that Russia is siding with the United States. Then on November 29, a Pravda editorial said:

. . . Imperialism is trying to capitalize on the weakened unity of Communist ranks. Those who refuse to cooperate and turn down proposals for joint action against the aggressors are hampering the struggle of the Vietnam people and helping the aggressor.

Finally, on November 30, Peking radio made the following comment on a book published in Moscow under the title *The USSR and the USA: Their Political and Economic Relations*—the book's purpose was "to preach the revisionist line of USSR-US cooperation for the domination of the world."

Whereas the Red Chinese have fomented extreme tactics in plot and conterplot, the Russians have tended to follow more familiar trade-and-aid policies. As in Indonesia and Zanzibar—and before that in Guinea—the Red Chinese have overplayed their hand and have been penalized by serious setbacks. Playing with small stakes, the Red Chinese can afford to take daring chances and play long shots far from home

By contrast, the Russian effort was epitomized by their activities in Ghana.[2] The pattern is familiar, beginning with a 1961 balance-of-payments crisis in Ghana. The Ghanaian government responded to the crisis by imposing strict import controls and increasing taxes, but this stopgap response had to

[2] An illuminating summary of the Russian effort has been reported in "Africa: Sales Frontier for U.S. Business," published in March 1963, as a supplement to *International Commerce*. See Evelyn M. Schwarztrauber, "Soviet Bloc Economic Offensive: Ghana, A Case Study," pp. 63–65, in the supplement.

be supplemented—in the longer run—by diversifying agriculture and establishing an industrial base. To achieve this, capital expenditures were needed for equipment, plants, mechanization of agriculture and technical aid. But a self-defeating cycle was involved: the balance-of-payments crisis made it difficult to obtain the financing that would make it possible to develop the country and forestall future crises.

The Soviet bloc responded with offers of capital loans on easy terms with low-interest rates. Exploratory trade missions were sent to Ghana as the Russians opened a permanent trade exhibit in Accra. Kwame Nkrumah, then President, toured the satellites in the summer of 1961, where the Communists impressed him with their industrial achievements. Next Ghanaian trade missions were sent to negotiate bilateral agreements. Symbolic of the growing relationship was the beginning of Soviet air service to Ghana in September 1962, and the opening of service to Moscow by Ghana Airways a few months later.

By early 1962, Ghana had signed bilateral trade and payment agreements with Soviet bloc countries totaling $196 million—about half of the total directly with Russia. The bloc had moved quickly, presenting proposals for grandiose projects in both industry and agriculture. The growing contacts were reflected in the trade figures by mid-1962: exports to Russia practically increased fivefold over the same six-month period a year earlier, imports increased 35 percent. Meanwhile, cocoa shipments to the United States dropped sharply, producing a 30 percent decline in exports in the first half of 1962 compared with 1961, and imports from the United States dropped 23 percent. Thus, in a short period, the Soviet bloc policy of trade and aid had paid dividends.

At the same time, the Russians were at a disadvantage in competing with the West in technical know-how and equipment. Ideology aside, a trade-and-aid policy depends on economics and efficiency. In Ghana, as elsewhere in the Afro-Asian world, the Soviet drawbacks became evident. When agreements with the Soviet bloc were examined in terms of comparable Western projects, they were found to be more expensive. Moreover, Soviet bloc equipment was generally found to be unsatisfactory. For example, six out of eight Ilyushin 18's had to be withdrawn from West Africa air routes because they were too expensive to operate. They were replaced with Viscount Aircraft. Moreover, deliveries were slow and often unsuitable material was shipped.

On the other hand, aid from the West appears hedged by too many "financial" conditions. Afro-Asian leaders look westward for assistance and too often encounter the prudent banker, rather than the enlightened expert prepared to take a chance. Moreover, the cultural and psychological context is too easily ignored by the Westerner approaching an underdeveloped country. Nor is contact with the Afro-Asians promoted by the self-serving political arguments in the West about foreign aid and "gratitude."

Most of all, both East and West persist in seeing the world as the battleground for their ideological, political and diplomatic contest. These are the terms in which the Communists, in particular, interpret all Western actions, while they see themselves as liberators. The coinage of labels is so debased that the Communists ignore the role of latter-day imperialists which they have assumed. That the Russians invariably revert to this distorted view was once again demonstrated by the famous interview of Premier Aleksei N. Kosygin by James Reston of *The New York Times*. "Now, just look at the world situation," Mr. Kosygin said. "Everywhere the United States is lending its support to the colonialists, to the side of the oppressors, not the oppressed." He then charged that the

United States does not want the people of the world "to rise up for their freedom." The date of the interview was ironic— December 7, 1965—24 years after Pearl Harbor, as Mr. Kosygin's words followed the dreadful dialogue of Cold War: "It is the United States which is setting the military tone and whipping up military psychosis. It is of your doing, this generating of tensions in the world."

It is at this point that the three-way division of the world must be approached with caution. It is the way the world is seen by the two powerful protagonists of East and West. The Third World has a different aim and seeks a different victory. Whereas Communists look to their day of ultimate victory and the free world operates with belief in the ultimate triumph of freedom and democracy, the emerging nations are concerned about victory measured in progress. Afro-Asian leaders have the darkness of illiteracy to dispel, the whirlwind of disease and pestilence to quell, the ravages of hunger to weather. This is not victory in geopolitical terms nor in the sophisticated geometry of traditional diplomacy. It is the march toward national development and the demand for revolution in the conditions of human life.

This aim is fused with an intense love of homeland and the searing nationalism that springs from it. Among all the self-defeating examples of ethnocentrism that both East and West can demonstrate, the failure to grasp Afro-Asian patriotism is one of the most crippling. Their patriotism can be found in the writings and statements of Afro-Asian nationalist leaders and it can be experienced in dealings with them. When encountered—as I have encountered it in repeated travels to the new nations—it provides a memorable and penetrating insight into the Afro-Asian world.

One of Africa's most eloquent voices, Senegalese President Léopold Sédar Senghor, described this patriotism in a 1961 address to Fordham University students:

Like yourselves, the young people of Black Africa are in the process of preparing their arms, of forming their minds in the disciplines which now govern the world. They have a keen consciousness of their "situation." Living in a country which is now in the process of being developed, their action has a double meaning: to follow closely the present reality and to look into the future. By so doing, they will have remained faithful to the tradition of their people. Our young people know that it is impossible for them to remain idle, apart from the great movement of history. They know that nature can be tamed, that the means offered by a technical civilization can be of great help to them. The tasks which confront them are, indeed, staggering. But from the education of children to the creation of a road system, the process is essentially the same. No one will speak henceforth of Promethean projects but what is being achieved now in the fully developed countries thanks to scientific methods and technical means deserves to retain our attention.

When the revered Zulu chief, Albert John Luthuli, received the Nobel Peace Prize in 1961, he set forth the "single aim" of all Africa: "Our goal is a united Africa in which the standards of life and liberty are constantly expanding; in which the ancient legacy of illiteracy and disease is swept aside, in which the dignity of man is rescued from beneath the heels of colonialism which have trampled it."

In his autobiography, Jawaharlal Nehru changed the locale to Asia, but the fire of patriotism is no less intense:

Yet India with all her poverty and degradation had enough of nobility and greatness about her; and, though she was over-burdened with ancient tradition and present misery and her eyelids were a little weary, she had "a beauty wrought out from within upon the flesh, the deposit, little cell by cell, of strange thoughts and fantastic reveries and exquisite passions." Behind and within her battered body one could still glimpse a majesty of soul.[3]

These statements, widely separated, point out the impact of patriotism within the Third World of nations. It is the emotional motive power for the drive toward national develop-

[3] Jawaharlal Nehru, *Toward Freedom* (New York: John Day, 1941), p. 271.

ment and it is an overwhelming psychological influence upon those nations who are neither in the Western nor the Eastern camps. They have a task that has chosen them: the raising of their country to modern nationhood.

While division of the world into a tripartite power structure determines and explains power politics, it must not becloud the division into two views and two perspectives. On one hand, East and West see the problem of power and ultimate political victory; on the other hand, the Third World is preoccupied with national development. This preoccupation and patriotism must be kept in the foreground in examining Western policy and the Third World.

CHAPTER THREE

HISTORICAL DEVELOPMENT

OF WESTERN POLICY

Western policy in the Afro-Asian world originated with the notion that the rest of the world was a rich, promising field to be cultivated for the benefit of Europe. The Westerner as cultivator was exploiter, tyrant, trader, teacher, missionary, builder and destroyer, partner and overlord, friend and foe. Yet amidst a certain amount of ambivalence, the paramount theme was unequivocal: the European arrived in faraway places to serve the interests of the flag he planted in the soil. He moved along the shores of Africa, advancing across the Atlantic to North and South America, establishing contacts along the coasts of India, China and the Philippines, always serving the interests of the Western power concerned.

When a Western power moved into an Afro-Asian area, the wide range of its society became involved, creating a network of vested interests. The sequence was familiar: first the traders, then the soldiers, followed by civilians who settled and stabilized the Western presence. The churches came both to

31

minister to their fellow countrymen and to convert the non-believing natives.

Whereas South America broke its colonial connections with Spain early in the nineteenth century, the domination of the Afro-Asian world by the West was at its height when World War I began. The domination was complete—political, economic and social. Its overriding theme was the superiority of the white European "way of life"; Afro-Asians were evaluated in terms of how they performed according to the white Western ethic. This domination remained in force through World War II.

During this period the sustained impact of the West was to surround every aspect of Western life with an aura of superiority. An intrinsic part of this domination was the affluence of the West vis-à-vis the peoples of color whose poverty was overwhelming, with little hope for change. This socio-economic degradation, along with Western political subjugation, resulted in a psychological climate of master-servant. This was so strong and so sustained that it will be a significant factor for some time in relationships between the West and the Third World.

The significance of the period of Western domination on the current attitudes of the Afro-Asian peoples is reflected in the fact that the present decision-makers in the Third World have experienced the master-servant syndrome imposed by the West.

GENERATIONS

Age Bracket in 1966	Born
46 to 66	1900 to 1920
26 to 46	1920 to 1940
16 to 26	1940 to 1950

These Afro-Asians now 46 to 66 years of age saw the West as absolute master with little hope of change during their youth and adulthood. The 26-to-46-year-old group, from which the leadership of many Third World countries now comes, spent their formative years in this relationship. The youngest group had few years of direct experience, but were influenced by the attitudes of their grandfathers and fathers.

Generally speaking, since 1900 the relationships between Afro-Asians and their European overlords were free from bloodshed and open war. But the leadership groups in the Afro-Asian countries still have the taste of domination, and their resentment lingers in one way or another. In recent years, the sustained influence of such experiences has been evident in the belated reactions to British domination of the Irish, Anglo-Canadian domination of the French Canadians and Spanish domination of the Netherlands. It will not be any different with the Afro-Asians.

There is an added ingredient and a formidable difference between the Afro-Asian memory of the West and the Irish memory of the British. It is race. The peoples of color were dominated by white peoples and made to feel that they were inferior because they were not white.

It was against this background that the process of political change went into high gear after World War II. Some observers have felt that the peaceful turning over of power by the Western powers to the Afro-Asian peoples would soon blot out the memories of domination and subjugation of the peoples of color.

But, as a good friend of the West, Carlos Romulo of the Philippines, pointed out, the impact was too pervasive, too prolonged to be blown away by "winds of change":

there has not been and there is not a Western colonial regime, which has not imposed, to a greater or lesser degree, on the people it ruled, a doctrine of their own racial inferiority. We have known and some of us still know, the searing experience of being demeaned in our own lands, of being systematically relegated to subject status not only politically and economically and militarily—but racially as well. Here was a stigma that could be applied to rich and poor alike, to prince and slave, bossman and workingman, landlord and peasant, scholar and ignoramus. To bolster his rule, to justify his own power to himself, Western white man assumed that his superiority lay in his very genes, in the color of his skin. This made the lowest drunken sot superior, in colonial society, to the highest product of culture and scholarship among the subject people.[1]

Thus the main residual impact of the former Western domination of the Third World is racialism, a complex phenomenon that encompasses every aspect of a person's personality and every area of a society. Non-white contact with white in the colonial era was a humiliating experience which left a deep and abiding scar. In *The Third World,* Mario Rossi has pointed out that a connection can be made between the colonial era and today's world in terms of racialism and other forms of inequality. Rossi has described a latter-day manifestation in international affairs: the Third World sees the reappearance of colonialism when the West denies to Asians and Africans the dignity of equals—not only man-to-man, but also nation-to-nation—by not taking into sufficient account the views and aspirations of the emerging countries and by acting as though Europe and North America were the center of the world.

It is another form of the ethnocentrism, the cultural narrowness with which the West viewed the non-Western world. In the perspective of centuries—rather than decades—the West has scant basis for claiming cultural superiority. In the more than two thousand years in which East and West have been in contact to varying degrees, progress, culture and

[1] Address of Carlos Romulo, Bandung Conference, 1955.

civilization flowered in India and China long before the Christian era in the West. When contacts between Europe and Asia were minimal, it was Europe, not Asia, that was undergoing a "dark age."

For its part, the United States has a historic dependency on the East. It was the search for new trade routes to Asia that brought Magellan and Columbus to America. Then, after the American Revolution, it was the lucrative China trade that enabled our Atlantic seaports to flourish and New England fortunes to emerge.

It was trade, too, that personified the heritage of superiority-inferiority in Western contact with the Afro-Asian world. It was the infamous "three-cornered trade" in which one corner consisted of humans who were not white. It was the slave trade in which iron bars, materials and shoddy goods were shipped from a European port and sold in West Africa. Then a cargo of "ebony" left for the West Indies of Louisiana. The return journey was made with a cargo of rum or sugar.

In the course of 350 years, from 1518 to 1865, the Atlantic slave trade cost between thirty and forty million lives. At least fifteen million Africans crossed the ocean in a grisly record which brutalized all who took part. The human ingredients were forgotten. The Africans were black cargo to be delivered in salable condition. They were purchased by slavers from native merchants as Africans fought Africans and captured slaves—to be sold for consumer goods and muskets.

For the visitor to Africa, the symbol of this cruel exchange is a small windswept island off Senegal's capital city of Dakar. Until 1617, when the Dutch bought the island for the price of a few iron bars, it was called the Isle of Ber. Then it became Gorée and soon it was a storage place for human beings sold into slavery. In the slave depots of Gorée, Africans were stored until the ships arrived to take them away. Still standing on Gorée Island is the "Slave House," built between 1776 and 1778, a reminder of the bizarre function once filled by an isolated piece of land off the west coast of Africa.

Asia, which was spared this notorious page in the Western presence in Afro-Asian affairs, encountered the colonialism of conventional trade activity. This was epitomized by the English East India Company and the Dutch East India Company founded in the early 1600s. The British target was India, while the Dutch became involved in Java and the Spice Islands. The Portuguese were already there, having virtually dominated the Indian Ocean trade from coastal outposts. The French came onto the scene in the 1660s with the Company of the Indies. While the English gained supremacy in India in 1818, the colonial period in Southeast Asia formed a relatively short chapter, considering the area's long history. Colonialism did not really get started in Southeast Asia as a systematic planned process until 1870. Then it lasted only about seventy years.

Under the Manchu dynasty, the Chinese Empire resembled a system of international relationships rather than a state as known in the West. Various foreign powers—Britain, France, Germany and Czarist Russia—had agreements with the Empire to pursue trade. These commercial ties came into existence only after the Opium War of 1840 through which victorious Britain forced China into definite trade relations with the rest of the world.

Defeated and humiliated in the War, China concluded peace with Britain under heavy penalties. By the Treaty of Nanking, in August of 1842, she was compelled to open five ports to foreign trade. Among these were Canton, Amoy and Shanghai. Furthermore, she ceded the island of Hong Kong to Britain in perpetuity and had to pay a war indemnity of $21 million. This sum included compensation for damage done to British opium in Canton in 1839.

After the defeat by Britain, China extended similar trade rights to France and the United States. In 1844, Caleb Cushing won favorable terms for the United States. But Britain remained the dominant foreign power. According to the former United States diplomat, George Kennan, Britain controlled 80 percent of the Chinese trade, which was concentrated in the Yangtze Valley. The other powers combined shared the remaining 20 percent.[2] Because of this favorable position, Britain understandably advocated the so-called "Open Door" policy in China. All participants in this trade had to be equal in customs treatment and harbor dues for the importation of merchandise for consumption purposes.

To the mass of the Chinese people, the weakness of their country in the face of foreign incursions was not apparent. It was the Sino-Japanese War of 1895 that opened their eyes. After this war, which they had regarded as an act of folly by the Manchus, they were forced to pay Japan a huge indemnity. In a desperate move to rid themselves of foreign domination and to regain their old respect, they rose in what is now known as the Boxer Rebellion of 1900, which was unsuccessful.

The war with Japan was merely the immediate spark of the Rebellion. Previously there had been simmering discontent with the activities of the European powers. Their territorial aggressions were the underlying cause. France, Germany and Russia entered the war on China's side. But she had to pay the price of their help. Soon Russia had made an agreement, the Cassini Convention, which gave her enormous trade privileges —railways and also Port Arthur. This Convention prompted France and Germany to send armed forces to stake their claims.

[2] George F. Kennan, *American Diplomacy 1900–1950* (New York: New American Library, 1951), p. 26. A useful source on China and the West is G. N. Steiger, *China and the Occident: The Origin and Development of the Boxer Movement* (New Haven: Yale University Press, 1927).

The Boxer Rebellion having failed, China was further parceled out among the victors. Russia used it to strengthen her hold on Manchuria, while the indemnities on China forced her to borrow increasingly from the other powers. In this way, she became heavily dependent on them.

This humiliation of China is largely responsible for the conversion to Marxism of Mao Tse-tung and his colleagues. It also explains their present efforts to make China once more a mighty force in the world.

The colonial race for Africa began about the same time as in Southeast Asia and was virtually settled by 1898. The Berlin Conference of 1844–85 set the ground rules for the European adventure in Africa. Britain and France competed for the Sudan, Britain and Germany for the Cameroons. All Africa was the prize and by the beginning of this century Africa was shared by Great Britain, France, Belgium, Italy, Portugal, Spain and Germany.

This dominance of the West was more profound in Africa than in Asia. Asia was not cut up or balkanized into as many colonies and spheres of influence as Africa. The explanation lies in the fact that while in Asia the bigger powers tended to eliminate the smaller ones, in Africa even minor countries got portions as consolation prizes. Hence the plethora of states today. Many of them consist of the same ethnic groups and for this very reason ought to be able to merge. But their divergent colonial heritages tend to militate against such unity.

In the mid-twentieth century, the size and extent of the domination of Africa seemed incredible. Never have so many and so much been in the hands of so few. In the 1950s, the total white European population of Africa was five million, compared with 193 million Africans. Except for the 2.5 million Europeans in South Africa and the 1.6 million in French North Africa, Africa was controlled by about one million white Europeans!

The colonial approach of each European power varied from place to place. The British, using indirect rule, administered through the mechanism of native leaders and operated under an official policy of preparing local populations for self-government within the Commonwealth. In the pre-independence era, the British were busily preparing—in stages—for self-government, though complaints were widespread that the stages were too slow. It is worth noting that in the past four hundred years more than one hundred colonies have been established by people from the British Isles, including, of course, the American colonies. Rather than rule by force indefinitely, the British changed their policy to national freedom, without losing political and economic advantages.

After World War II, W. Hardy Wickwar wrote of the Commonwealth experience: " 'Functionalism, not federalism' is the standard practice of British countries in dealing with one another. Current British stress on consultation among all interested parties, as the very essence of democracy, is also reinforced by the experience of the Commonwealth, for this community of nations is based upon consensus, compromise, respect, and tolerance."[3]

By contrast, the French sought to convert Africans into black Frenchmen. Their rule was direct, which explains the large number of French administrative personnel in Africa. In prewar West Africa, the French governed a population five-eighths the size of that ruled by Britain, but used three times as many administrators—31,000 to 11,000. France sought to immerse Africans in French language and culture. Paris was the mecca, French civilization the apex. Black Africans were citizens of France and their representatives sat in the French Parliament.

[3] W. Hardy Wickwar, "From Empire to Commonwealth," in *Foreign Governments: The Dynamics of Politics Abroad,* Fritz Morstein Marx, ed. (New York: Prentice-Hall, Inc., 1949), p. 156.

Under Belgian colonial rule, economic benefits were offered while political opportunities were withheld. Not even Belgians could vote in the Congo. In such a context, it was not surprising that the Belgians were blind to the forces of nationalism in Africa. Their view was economic and so were their solutions. But in the Congo, the disaster was political and governmental.

Outright exploitation has characterized Portuguese policy. Determined to maintain what has now become an impossible status quo, the Portuguese had kept the African in a world of ignorance and isolation. Their repressive rule provided one innovation: the *assimilado* or *civilizado* system. Under law, an African who passed certain tests became, in effect, a white man as far as Portuguese administrators were concerned. But it was a cruel fiction. After more than 500 years in Africa, the Portuguese had, according to the 1950 census, 30,039 assimilado Africans out of 4 million in Angola and 4,353 out of 5.7 million in Mozambique.

In any accounting of the historical background of Western policy in the Afro-Asian world, the results of colonialism show dramatically that the West reaped a rich harvest. The merchant shipping of France, England and the Netherlands profited from the slave trade and new industries were provided with markets abroad. The primary capital that was generated was invested in mines, railways and cotton mills. In the Western Hemisphere, the human cargoes contributed in large measure to the settlement of two continents.

The pattern of exploitation under colonialism translated the master-servant relationship onto the economic level. The colonies were operated for the benefit of the home country. The moral crime of slavery was accompanied by political and economic exploitation. Margery Perham has written that slavery was "one unalleviated, questionable, widespread, long-continuing and highly profitable crime."[4] It can also be said that colonialism was an enduring, self-serving and highly profitable form of exploitation.

The result, from the Afro-Asian viewpoint, was a bitter harvest. The rich Western nations had become richer at their expense, and thus they increased the gap between the rich nations and the poor ones. In the post-World War II era, this gap has developed a particular urgency as the former colonial areas have become independent. As mankind approaches 1970, all of the Afro-Asian areas once occupied by the Western powers are independent—with the exception of southern Africa and a few scattered vestiges of nineteenth-century colonial domination.

The historical development of Western control of the Afro-Asian peoples was rooted in legal-political domination and the implied superiority of white European culture. While legal-political control has come to an end in most Afro-Asian countries, the racial attitudes of the former colonial powers have left a deep impact. The racial impact remains a vital factor in the Western–Third World equation.

Only a drastic change in Western attitudes on race will convince the Afro-Asian leadership that the West believes that all men are equal members of the human family. And there is no more towering challenge to the West's belief in the unity of man than the poverty, illiteracy and disease of the developing countries. The affluent West faces a Third World haunted by the unholy trio as well as memories of colonialism.

[4] Margery Perham, *The Colonial Reckoning* (New York: Alfred A. Knopf, Inc., 1961), p. 129.

CHAPTER FOUR

VITAL ELEMENTS IN THE
AFRO-ASIAN COMPLEX—
A DANGEROUS GAP,
A DESPERATE UNITY

The Diary of Carolina Maria de Jesus begins this way:

The birthday of my daughter Vera Eunice. I wanted to buy a pair of shoes for her, but the price of food keeps us from realizing our desires. Actually we are slaves to the cost of living. I found a pair of shoes in the garbage, washed them, and patched them for her to wear.[1]

It is the diary of a Negro mother living in the slums of Brazil, but it speaks for the majority of the human race by reflecting the desperate condition of the non-white world. Hunger stalks across the pages of the diary. So do poverty,

[1] *Child of the Dark: The Diary of Carolina Maria de Jesus,* translated by David St. Clair (New York: E. P. Dutton and Co., 1962), p. 19.

42

disease and illiteracy. But in this case a voice cried out from the depths, ending the silence of the depressed, for Carolina Maria de Jesus, simple and uneducated, was able to put down in writing what the world's poor experience in mute suffering.

A response—one of many uttered since the end of World War II—could be heard on a summer's day in Omaha, when President Johnson said on June 30, 1966: "If the strong and the wealthy turn from the needs of the weak and the poor, frustration is sure to be followed by force. No peace and no power is strong enough to stand for long against the restless discontent of millions of human beings who are without any hope."

A warning—one of many uttered since the end of World War II—was sounded by United Nations Secretary-General U Thant in a statement introducing his annual report in the summer of 1962: "The present division of the world into rich and poor countries is . . . much more real and much more serious, and ultimately much more explosive, than the division of the world on ideological grounds."

At the grass roots, human suffering; at the summit, awareness, pleas and warnings. The West looks across a dangerous gap of poverty and its dread corollaries of poverty, illiteracy and disease, and what the West sees is the majority of the human race collected into a Third World made up of non-whites. On the other side of that gap there is a desperate unity whose common denominator is deprivation, whose common hope is a life of human dignity.

The statistics of the gap are already grim with overtones of pending catastrophe. Based on the gross national product, the United States has a per capita income of $3,000 a year; Europe is at the $1,200–$1,800 level. The underdeveloped two-thirds of the world lives on an income of $100 per person—or less.

What of the immediate future? One pessimistic projection follows another. For instance, calculations have been made from the $6 billion a year in assistance provided by the governments of the industrial nations, assuming the most efficient use of funds and allowing for loan repayments that do not cut into new funds. Economists figure that the maximum achievable increase from the $6 billion annual aid would be 5 percent per year. At such a rate of increase and with the present rates at which population is growing, it would take about twenty-five years just to double the $100 level in the developing countries constituting the Third World.

According to economists, three to four dollars of capital investment are required to increase a nation's gross income by one dollar. India alone might need $15 billion a year in aid— instead of the $1.8 billion it received in 1964—merely to double its $80 per capita income by 1975.

The outlook is clouded further by the fiscal storms gathering over the underdeveloped countries. Their debts are growing faster than their ability to pay. In 1955, the underdeveloped countries were in debt a total of $10 billion—7 percent of their gross national product. Ten years later, their debt had become $30 billion—15 percent of their gross national product.

The magnitude of the task requires a major miracle, according to Carl Kaysen, who was deputy special assistant to the President for National Security Affairs and now has resumed his University career. He has raised the perilous question that Americans must answer:

Does the rich one-third of the world really want to live in a world where it continues to get richer and where the poor two-thirds remain miserably poor and largely illiterate? Can a nation that "feels" be happy in a world like that?[2]

2 Interview in *Christian Science Monitor*, December 28, 1965.

Professor Kaysen has answered for all Americans—as has President Johnson. A lasting peace that transcends the nuclear stalemate, and the bridging of the gap between the rich and poor nations are the great challenges facing America. "These are so much bigger than all the rest of the problems. I don't know how we are going to get them done. But we must."

In thirty-five years, there will be between six and seven billion mouths to feed in the world; in that time alone, the world must make room for an additional billion Chinese. With the doubling of the world's population by the end of this century, famine becomes a frightening and very real prospect. The world food supply must be increased by one-third just to prevent the aching plight of two billion hungry humans from getting worse.

Just over the horizon, the gap between rich and poor, "have" and "have-not" nations increases rather than decreases. As President Johnson reminded the nation and the world in his Omaha speech:

Here today in the center of the greatest food-producing area anywhere on this globe, we Americans must face a sobering fact: Most of the world's population is losing the battle to feed itself. And if present trends continue we can now see the point at which even our own vast resources, including the millions of acres that we now hold in reserve, will not be sufficient to meet the requirements of human beings for food.

Even Latin America, which has better prospects than the Afro-Asian countries, increased food output by only 6 percent in the past five years while population rose 11 percent. At the same time, the opposite was occurring in Europe, where food production increased by 11 percent and population rose only 4 percent. In the area of income, the gap increases with the same menacing aspects. In another decade, the per capita income of the "have" nations will be about $4,000 per year compared with only $800 a year among the "have-not" nations.

In such a context, the deprived nations of the Third World constitute a common front against poverty and deprivation. Comparisons can be cruel, particularly when the "have-nots" see East and West pouring $120 billion each year into military spending. The United States is spending $20 billion alone on landing a man on the moon. Meanwhile, leaders in Africa and Asia confront in their streets babies dead from malnutrition, children with stomachs bloated by hunger, adults old and dying before forty—the age when life "begins" in the Western world.

Even though the total flow of aid to the less developed countries from the industrial West reached record levels in 1965, the figure was less than 1 percent (0.85%) of their gross national product. A total of $10.98 billion in aid flowed from public and private sources, up $1 billion from 1964. Here is where the aid came from:

—Bilateral government aid from the fifteen industrial countries comprising the Development Assistance Committee, an arm of the Organization for Economic Cooperation and Development, with headquarters in Paris. This totaled $5.8 billion, including food shipments by the United States.

—Private capital totaling $3.6 billion. This included investments in mines and factories and exports on credit terms with more than one year to pay, usually guaranteed by governments.

—Aid from the Communist countries totaling about $670 million.

In the total of $10.98 billion, the United States has the lion's share of $4 billion out of the $5.8 million provided by governments. Leaders in the Third World—from the despairing vantage point of national poverty—can make comparisons that Americans will regard as misleading and as distorted. But the emotional and psychological impact of comparison remains powerful: four times as much spent on sending a man to the moon as for the catastrophic needs of the Third World. Billions for destruction, but only millions for food.

Yet when responsible leaders of the Third World confront Americans, they speak more in sadness than anger. A striking example is the writer-diplomat of Senegal, Ousmane Soce Diop, who traveled to Illinois to remind a campus audience:

We must remember that before the end of this century, the world's population will have doubled due to the magnitude of the present population explosion, and that the world of the year 2000 will be an extraordinary world in which one man out of every two will be an Asian, and where three-fourths of the non-Asians will be from underdeveloped countries. Thus, seven-eighths of the world population will be composed of men living in underfed countries, in ignorance, sickness, and poverty. In contrast, there will be one-eighth of the human population living in the industrialized countries, highly developed, with 90 percent of the world's resources in their hands and a correspondingly high standard of living. That is the disturbing view of the world in the next quarter-century, a world off balance where, with every passing day, the rich get richer, and the poor poorer and more numerous. The impasse and the danger are well known. They have been studied by competent experts who have weighed them to the nearest gram and measured them to the nearest millimeter, but despite the great alarm which was sounded in Geneva in the spring of 1964 during the United Nations Conference on Trade and Development, no positive step has yet been taken. One has the impression that our contemporary world is marching toward the final impasse, the apocalypse, impelled by the same Fate which struck the hero of the ancient Greek tragedy. He advanced step by step, closer and closer to death, fully aware of what he was doing but unable to stop himself. The chorus of spectators, as powerless as he, could only cry "alas" in sympathy.[3]

[3] Address of the Ambassador of the Republic of Senegal, Ousmane Soce Diop, to the University of Carbondale, Illinois, October 21, 1965.

Thus, the emotions and the economics of the poverty of nations produce psychological attitudes and practical impera- tives that are felt in the Third World and transmitted to the West. A unity of demand, of intention and of urgency has emerged along with the new nationalisms and the new free- doms. The Third World stands united in its "have-not" posi- tion, a victim of deprivation. Yet time, numbers and needs are on the side of the so-called victims, for the "haves" cannot ignore them. The question is whether the response will be massive enough, effective enough, soon enough to avoid global catastrophe.

An unfamiliar factor has been added to international affairs, a factor unknown to the world of Disraeli, Western colonizers and gunboat diplomats. Power no longer can com- pel. While the "have-not" nations lack power, the "haves" are not free to use their power to compel, to order and to have their way. The standoff between East and West dramatizes the futility of power. In another day, it was said that power corrupts. Today, power inhibits. Presidents, premiers and prime ministers of the world's leading countries stop to under- stand, listen to comprehend, look to see. The world is no longer of their making and they must labor to prevent the outcome from endangering the powerful few nations. It is more than easy rhetoric to say that no man, no country is an island. The world has become a global village.

When the West confronts the Third World and the unifying imperative of poverty, it must accept the desire to modernize as fundamental—rather than any inclination to westernize. The Afro-Asians are operating within their own social- cultural-economic matrix, and it is this matrix that gives shape to their unity in poverty.

Afro-Asians are villagers in a special sense. While com- munications have made the world a global village, Western man is urban, impersonal, achievement-oriented, pragmatic, competitive. Psychologically, the Afro-Asian remains a villager. He is most at ease with face-to-face contacts, with well-established relationships, with clear personal mandates and fixed social responsibilities.

Western man too easily miscalculates the relationship tween poverty and the village mentality, and between abundance and the urban, industrial mentality. The social conditions prevalent in the Third World "have-nots" are inextricably bound to the realities. Lacking economic sufficiency, unable to provide opportunities for advancement, finding it necessary to avoid social competition in a system that could only provide rewards for the few rather than the many, such societies work in traditional ways. Fixed patterns, inherited position, resistance to change have provided the wherewithal for internal stability and domestic tranquillity.

In his penetrating study, *People of Plenty,* David M. Potter has related this to the problem of exporting democracy—a facile, often misleading and sometimes self-defeating campaign that has been mistaken for a realistic, viable and effective policy in dealing with the Third World. Potter points out that "when we propose world-wide adoption of democracy, our problem is not merely to inspire a belief in it but to encourage conditions conducive to it."[4] Again, the unavoidable confrontation with poverty and the need to provide the means of economic development.

Here the West is confronted with both ideological and practical problems. On one hand, the problem of understanding the guiding philosophies prevalent among the governments and leaders in the Third World; on the other, the problem of

---

[4] David M. Potter, *People of Plenty, Economic Abundance and the American Character* (Chicago: University of Chicago Press, Phoenix Books, 1958), p. 117.

providing the practical means for development—in social, economic, fiscal, technical areas. In both the ideological and the practical confrontation with poverty in the Third World, the West must outlive and overcome the heritage of white supremacy.

It is a lingering myth that remains dangerous, though it has gone underground. Except for the remaining strongholds where this perverted myth is preached and practiced openly, Western man—and, for that matter, Communist man—verbalizes equality. Nonetheless, subliminal attitudes still infect relations between white and non-white across the poverty gap. The significance of the separation of rich and poor nations largely according to color cannot be ignored. A map of the world in which poverty and non-white are marked off shows the mischievous overlapping of the two.

Rich, privileged and white—these characteristics are associated with Western man in contact with the poor, deprived and non-white world. White and non-white still run the risk of perceiving a superior-inferior dimension: the white man seeming to view and, in certain instances, actually seeing the non-white as inferior; and the non-white sensitive to such attitudes, even to the extent of perceiving them at times when they do not exist. This barrier to understanding remains a possibility whenever white confronts yellow, brown or black man, whenever the helped and the helper are consistently distinguishable on the basis of color.

Yet the problem of color is distinct from the practical problems of development: the need for an infra-structure of communications, financing and know-how. A developing country needs to develop an efficient organization of production and distribution. Roads, railways and airlines are needed. Storage and sales machinery must be coordinated; barter must yield to cash and credit. These are the problems of the economist, but their solutions also require the sensitivity of the social psychologist, for the Third World countries cannot and will not abandon their customs and mores in a blind, wholesale exchange for the apparatus of development.

There is always the danger that the West—offering more efficient techniques—may contaminate their application by ignoring the Afro-Asian context. Or the Afro-Asian may discern another manifestation of white superiority. More than anything, the great contribution of the Peace Corps has been its handling of this threat to mutual understanding and acceptance. The theme of partnership and of sharing—rather than of dominance and condescension—has permeated the Peace Corps in an emphatic demonstration that the West can achieve fundamental rapport with the non-white world.

For its part, the Third World has a rendezvous with change. The struggle up from poverty involves major surgery, fundamental readjustments and widespread transformation of its societies. There must be acceptance of the difference between Westernization and modernization. If the West must realize the terms are not synonymous so must the Third World—and among its responsible and far-seeing leadership this enlightened attitude prevails.

Agriculture is the great frontier for Africa and Asia, for it is on the farm that progress will begin. It is there that the food problem is faced and also the cash and consumer problem solved for economies that must pass through significant intermediate steps before industrializing. The mass of the peasant populations in Asia and Africa—whose typical condition is the inefficient cultivation of land—hold the key to progress. The farm is the scene of the agricultural revolution that must take place. As L. Gray Cowan has observed:

Industrialization programs may provide a temporary palliative through a reduction of pressure on the land, but in the last analysis even these can only be successful if they go hand in hand with rural improvement programs designed to provide higher living standards for the mass of the peasants. Without this, the new consumer-goods industries will lack the mass market for their products, upon which their expansion depends. But modernization of the agricultural sector of the economy is perhaps everywhere the most difficult task of all, since it depends as much on a slow process of education as on the availability of capital.[5]

In both Asia and Africa, a balance is being sought between the social and psychological patterns associated with traditional ways and the traits that create and are created by modernization. In Asia, particularly, saving "face" is an important ingredient of daily life that faces the strain of an increasingly competitive economy. In both Africa and Asia, the commitment to family and clan often leads to unwieldy nepotism. The rural, village orientation of the masses—even after they move to the teeming cities—inhibits the drive toward achievement, though it by no means prevents the drive from developing. In the Afro-Asian exodus abroad to learn and the return to transform their native countries there is evidence of the growing stress on skill and professionalism.

Other characteristics of modernization are emerging, and their connection with the emergence from poverty cannot be ignored. A sensitivity to time, its importance and significance to production, is one example of a necessary trait. Willingness to substitute new ways for old—whether on the farm or in government office—produces a cumulative pattern of improvement. A sense of urgency, a concern for skill and a stress on performance are necessary for society to move forward; while the leadership circles manifest these traits, developing societies have to spread them throughout the population. Individual initiative, a willingness to take risks, self-reliance must be added. Above all, there must be a belief in progress.

[5] L. Gray Cowan, *The Dilemmas of African Independence* (New York: Walker and Company, 1964), p. 36.

This belief is present. The revolution of rising expectations, with its new-found confidence that "it can be done," represents both hope and threat for the leadership of the Third World countries.

Nor can the role of ideology be ignored. Short of capital, shorter still in entrepreneurship, private and public planning, the Third World countries must develop battle plans in the war against poverty. A passenger-train analogy used by Professor Potter pinpoints the problem of ways and means.[6] Passengers catching a "socialist" train would be seated by station attendants arbitrarily. People would be placed together without favor and there would be no adjustments made for those who like to sit near windows or away from ventilation. People could not expect to sit next to someone of their choice. At departure time, the train would be delayed until the attendants completed their preparations. The cost of train operations would be increased, passengers disconcerted and time-tables disrupted.

In a "democratic" train, those who wanted good seats would come early; those who did not care would come late. The passengers pick their seats, their neighbors and their locations. They distribute themselves throughout the train on their own without supervision, expense or delay. Of course, neither the "socialist" nor the "democratic" train analogy fits adequately as a description of how the respective systems operate. But one underlying assumption is pertinent to the operations of a democratic, free-enterprise economy: there must be enough seats for everyone. Otherwise, the unsupervised seating would lead to trouble on the train—just as uncontrolled competition for few rewards in an underdeveloped economy with limited resources would produce disruption and disputes.

[6] Potter, *op. cit.*, pp. 117–118.

In the nations of the Third World, where poverty rather than Western abundance is the guiding rule, forms of socialism carry great appeal. Nor is it a subversive word, even in the United States, where many government activities would be classified by Afro-Asians as manifestations of socialism. It is important to avoid simple labels and to apply terms cautiously. For the purposes of describing responses in the Third World to poverty and underdevelopment, types of socialism can be distinguished, bearing in mind that "most of the leaders of the newly-independent countries regard themselves as socialists of one type or another."[7] Throughout the Third World, there are self-styled Arab socialists, African socialists and Asian socialists. Westerners often forget that it is a "good" label among both leaders and followers in the Third World. To them, it means concern on the part of the government, expressed in active policies and programs to transform the nation and raise the living conditions.

Three different tendencies are discernible in Afro-Asian versions of socialism. First, there is the strongly Marxist orientation evident in such countries as North Korea and North Vietnam, which was evident in Indonesia under Sukarno and in Ghana under Nkrumah. With an emphasis on industrialization, a rejection of traditional attitudes toward economic practices and a strong leaning toward Moscow and Peking, such versions of socialism are Marxist in formulation and intent.

A second and moderate version of socialism is personified in the approach of President Senghor of Senegal. Balance and harmony are its hallmarks, a reasonable mixture of industrial and agricultural development, a blend of private and public investment, combined with a respect for traditional ways and

[7] I. R. Sinai, *The Challenge of Modernization* (New York: W. W. Norton & Co., 1964), p. 180.

a desire for measured innovation. According to Senghor, his version

draws upon the sources of humanism. It wants to liberate man (and all men) from economic and social shackles so as to allow him to fulfill himself. For this purpose, it wants to allow him to meet his basic needs, both material and spiritual. Its only condition is the effort to achieve the economic growth to bring production to the level of the needs. It is up to public authorities, based on men's consent, to direct this growth, in the name of the whole society, by making use of the greatest possible means of production and, if necessary, by accepting private means of production on the condition of controlling them, of ensuring submission to the general interest, even when safeguarding the legitimate interests of the owners. This effort to achieve growth will go hand in hand with a policy of social justice, which will reward the most active, even while giving priority to raising the standard of living of the most disinherited workers.

A third type of socialism can be described as the involvement of government in providing aid and assistance, but within traditional Afro-Asian contexts and without government ownership of the means of production. Emphasis is on proper use of wealth rather than on the facts of ownership and control. Observers might dismiss such an approach as not socialism at all. However, doctrinaire approaches are not of primary concern in the Third World countries. Each is following its own road up from poverty, and the labels are not paramount so long as what these countries cherish is not destroyed in their rendezvous with change.

It is at this point that the figure of Teilhard de Chardin emerges as the grand synthesizer in the worldwide struggle to give all men a life of dignity. The French Jesuit paleontologist and philosopher—with his view of a world progressing toward perfection—offers an overall approach that resonates throughout the planning and leadership circles of the Third World. Even where his theories are not espoused, they are applicable.

In keeping with his synthesizing role, Teilhard provides an
optimistic and intellectually compelling approach to the dangerous gap of poverty and the future unity that can emerge
in the world.

Teilhard views the variety in the world in terms of unification. Though in all of his scientific endeavors he sought to
differentiate one geological object from another, his very
acceptance of these differences led to his theory of union.
Teilhard felt that no real union can take place which does not
include differentiation. His concept of union extends to society
as a whole. He sees mankind converging; nations becoming
more interdependent, approaching a world community. He
asserts that mankind is now in a phase of socialization or
planetization in which men are becoming more collectivized
and more personalized, progressing toward that ultimate
union where man will be reconciled with man and finally with
God.

Yet Teilhard persistently affirms the preservation of differences. While one nation should not be smothered by another,
political and economic differences must not keep men from
uniting across arbitrary national barriers in a worldwide bond
of mutual action and love. He cites the common pursuit of the
human race and the unity which binds mankind. This socialization, the technical and spiritual organization of human
society, "does not in the least signify the end, but quite the
contrary the beginning on earth of the Era of the Person."

For Afro-Asians, this concept of union in which differences
are preserved is extremely meaningful. They are interested in
preserving their national personalities with all the traditions
and psychic and emotional tendencies born from vast historical backgrounds. Yet at the same time, they want to share the
benefits of modern technology and science developed in the
Western world. Most of the Afro-Asian leaders are eager to

join with the nations of the world in greater cooperation, especially in the economic and technological areas. They are interested, too, in developing more understanding between nations on a cultural and educational level.

Yet they do not wish to be considered completely helpless and void, receiving all and giving nothing to the rest of the world. Africans and Asians have something to contribute to mankind; they, too, have resources, both material and cultural, to communicate to the world. In Teilhard's concept of union, Afro-Asian leaders have seen the beginnings of a system of thought which would correspond to their own particular needs as they try desperately to overcome poverty.

All over the developing world there is a realization that a socialized society would not only be efficient economically, but that it would also build upon the traditional collectivity and common family life of the people. At the same time, national leaders have rejected the blind acceptance of one type of socialized system. They are, on the contrary, seeking to adapt ideas and form new methods that would be natural to their own traditions. There are differences in types of socialism practiced in the various developing countries, but practically all are seeking to preserve a value system centered on primary consideration for the human person and emphasizing the obligation of society to assume responsibility for his well-being. Therefore, a socialized system appeals to these leaders as the way to accomplish necessary progress.

In this context, Teilhard de Chardin offers a system which recognizes the necessity of the drawing together of men into a more tightly woven network, but a method "placing research and technology—political, economic, social and cultural—at the service of a pan-human socialization, of a World Civilization . . . the Humanism of our own times." Out of this, a future global unity can transcend the dangerous gap and the desperate unity of poverty.

TESTING GROUND FOR

SINO-SOVIET COMPETITION

As Trotsky said of Petrograd in October 1917, power is lying in the streets of the newly emergent Asian and African states—the Third World in international affairs. These nations, building upon a foundation of political independence, are in a state of transition toward complete independence in economic, social and diplomatic terms. Their leadership is a politically active minority governing masses of people who live on the streets of teeming cities and in the huts of tribal villages. For the Third World, it is a time of toil and trouble, of transition and testing; for the Communist forces of Russia and China, it is a time of temptation and trial, of opportunity and machination.

In the decade of the 1960s, as the red shadow began to lengthen across Africa, the variations, the strategy and the tactics in Communist policy epitomized the threat facing the Third World. In Africa, as Walter Laqueur has noted, the threat appeared with the sudden sound of a hammer and the sweep of a sickle:

58

Almost overnight Communism in Africa has become an international problem of the first magnitude. . . . Now in 1961, Africa has replaced the Middle East as the world's trouble center, and it is likely to remain the main area of contest between West and East for many years to come . . .[1]

However, as the situation developed, the contest was not limited to West and East; within the Communist bloc itself, Soviet Russia and Red China stood at cross purposes. This contest within a contest was never more vivid than in Africa in the mid-1960s, and thus a summary of this period is particularly revealing of the multiple role of Communism vis-à-vis the Third World and the multiple response thereby required of Western policy.

For the Russians, Communist policy is moving in a two-step paradigm of power strategy. The first step involves eviction of the West by removing its political influence, its economic opportunities and strategic bases. When he was Assistant Secretary of State for African Affairs, G. Mennen Williams summarized this first step by pointing out: "The principal thrust of Communist activities, at the present time and for the near future, continues to be destruction of the Western position in Africa and insinuating their way into African good graces by the establishment of an identity of Communist bloc–African positions on major international issues."[2]

During this first step—pursued by trade and aid, propaganda and politicking—the Soviet strategy has coincided with the struggle for complete independence in the developing countries. The Soviets have encouraged African nationalism —away from the West.

In the second and long-range step, the Communists have not abandoned their worldwide goal of domination. This

[1] Walter Laqueur, "Communism and Nationalism in Tropical Africa," *Foreign Affairs,* Vol. 39, No. 4 (July 1961), p. 610.
[2] G. Mennen Williams, "Communism's Impact on African Nationalism," *The Department of State Bulletin,* Vol. 48 (June 3, 1963), p. 877.

would involve emergence of Communist governments in the developing countries, regimes that would maintain themselves without Communist military occupation. Clearly, in a time when it has become increasingly difficult to maintain control in neighboring Soviet satellites even *with* a military presence, it would be impossible in the heart of a distant and very different continent.

Ironically, Soviet success in the first step endangers the success of the second step, because the Soviet paradigm lacks the inevitability with which the Communist dialectic likes to clothe itself. The emergent Afro-Asian nationalism, its leaders and its parties are moving toward independence of outside domination—of any kind, including Communist. The Soviets are in the frustrating position of trying the impossible—supporting independence from the West but not from themselves.

Meanwhile, in the first step, the Russians have made a considerable impact by exploiting the shibboleth of colonialism past and present. The Russians argue that "the colonialists never give away independence, and that people must win it in persistent struggle by force of arms or by other means and methods."[3] The Russian argument continues after independence by claiming that the West tries to keep Africa in a fragmented, balkanized condition. NATO is depicted, furthermore, as the agent of residual colonialism, and the finger of accusation is pointed at South Africa, Rhodesia and the Portuguese territories. It is charged that "Portugal's coffers and arsenals are being refilled by the major NATO countries, the USA above all."[4]

The argument is re-enforced on the economic level by the charge that the remaining white minority governments in

[3] Y. Konovalov, "Problems of Liberation of the Last Colonies in Africa," *International Affairs*, April 1964, p. 35.

[4] See Ivan Potekhin, "Pan-Africanism and the Struggle of the Two Ideologies," *International Affairs*, April 1964, p. 50.

Africa are linked to the West, particularly the United States and England, by their overseas investments. Here, the Russians—joined by several African leaders—demand drastic boycotts against South Africa, Rhodesia and the Portuguese territories. In an article titled "Who Trades With Apartheid?" the *African Review* (published in Ghana) summarized this feeling in June 1965, when it said that the Western powers "have rapidly increased their trade with South Africa in the postwar period, despite increasingly blatant South African apartheid policies and growing demands for a boycott on trade."

Paradoxically, the Red Chinese conduct a brisk trade with South Africa while simultaneously espousing the cause of African liberation. This one-sided trade consists in China's importation of corn and wool through intermediaries in Hong Kong. According to Colin Legum of *The Observer* of London, in 1962 China bought $15.75 million worth of these two commodities; in 1963 the figure tripled. He further remarks, "Trade has become so prominent that the Verwoerd government sent a trade commissioner there in 1963. His office sent booklets explaining the opportunities for trade with South Africa to all the P.R.C.'s (People's Republic of China) state-buying departments in November 1963."[5] China, of course, denies the existence of this trade and solemnly states that she has discontinued all her economic and commercial ties with the South African colonial authorities.

The Russians continued their African campaign with promises of economic aid. Between 1954 and 1962, the Russians offered an estimated $1 billion in aid to African countries. But the gap between promise and delivery was great indeed; only

---

[5] Colin Legum, "Africa and China, Symbol and Substance," in *Policies Toward China, Views from Six Continents,* edited by A. M. Halpern (New York: McGraw-Hill, for Council on Foreign Relations, 1965), p. 415.

$70 million was actually delivered in that period. By contrast, the United States promised about $2.25 billion and delivered $1.5 billion during the same period.

Soviet projects have been in the fields of agriculture, education, medicine, power, transportation, geological prospecting and housing. The two showcase projects of Soviet aid have been the controversial Aswan High Dam in the United Arab Republic and the atomic energy reactor in Ghana. The former project has been particularly stressed by Russia in the competition between Communism and capitalism, drawing on ill will created by the July 1956 withdrawal of financial support for the High Dam by the United States, Great Britain and the International Bank. At each stage of the High Dam's progress, Soviet representatives are highly visible and widely publicized participants in the ceremonies.

With another view to the future, the Russians opened Friendship University in Moscow in 1960. Its major target: the next generation of African leadership. African students have been a major part of the student body, symbolized by the renaming of the school as Patrice Lumumba University. For instance, in the 1962–63 school year, the United States had 5,000 students from Africa, but this number represented only 7 percent of the foreign students from underdeveloped countries. Russia had only 3,000 African students, representing 40 percent of their foreign students from the new nations.

African journalists have been another target. They have been given scholarships, and the Russians have sought to help African governments in setting up information and press agencies. In 1961 journalists from Ghana, Guinea, Upper Volta, Zanzibar, Mali, Algeria and Cameroon attended a conference of the Communist's International Organization of Journalists (IOJ) in Bamako. At that time, the All-African Journalist Union was established to "struggle against colonial-

ism, imperialism, and neo-colonialism and in favor of peace."
It was a familiar ploy.

Nor have fronts and movements been overlooked. The
Soviet-African Friendship Association was formed in 1959 to
arrange exhibitions, meetings, social events and other similar
activities. Friendship societies were soon organized in individual states, including Togo, Guinea, Mali, Senegal and
Sudan. Also, rallies and conventions have been sponsored
both in the Soviet Union and in Africa, keeping up the flow of
traffic between Russia and Africa.

In approaching the African trade movement, the Russians
have attempted to exert influence at the top rather than at the
grass roots. They have made overtures in trade union politics
and in international labor affiliation. Until the formation of
the All-African Trade Union Federation (AATUF) in 1961,
African unions were torn between the Communist-run World
Federation of Trade Unions (WFTU) and the Western-
oriented International Confederation of Free Trade Unions
(ICFTU). The Russian support of WFTU was accompanied
by predictable attacks upon the ICFTU and a lukewarm
attitude toward the AATUF—considered a threat in that it
drew the African unions into a separate and neutral orbit. In
addition, a new university was set up in Moscow to "cater" to
African trade unionists.

But Africa has by no means been the setting for a dramatic
Soviet success story. As noted in Chapter Two, Ghana was an
example both of successful overtures and of disappointments.
The Russians have frequently mismanaged and miscalculated
on a small as well as large scale. A large state rice farm in
Guinea was a failure. A shipload of cement arrived in a West
African port during the rainy season and was hardened
cement by the time trucks arrived to transport the cargo.
Despite the High Dam flurry, UAR President Nasser has put

local Communists in jail. The favored Sekou Touré of Guinea accused the Russians of conspiring to overthrow his government and expelled the Soviet Ambassador, Daniel Solod.

The small headway made by Communist parties in Africa is epitomized by the fact that Touré praised Soviet skills on one hand and then forbade members of his party to become Communists. Throughout Africa only a few Communist parties exist, concentrated mainly at the northern and southern ends of the continent. As noted by Kremlinologist Alexander Dallin, "Indeed, by 1963 all Communist parties in Africa were illegal, and none seemed to be faring well."[6]

Parallel setbacks have been encountered by Soviet overtures toward African trade unionism. Many union leaders in Africa have spoken out against the Communist-supported unions, and in such heavily unionized areas as Nigeria, the Congo and Rhodesia, the Communists have made few inroads. Among the students brought to Moscow for studies, there have been repeated outcries against Russian color bias and repressive treatment. Professor Robert A. Scalapino has commented that "relatively few Africans have thus far returned from the Communist world as enthusiastic supporters of the system."[7]

Besides the embarrassing gap between promise and delivery of aid, Russian efforts to develop trade with sub-Saharan Africa have not constituted a threat. In 1961, such trade amounted to less than 1 percent of total Soviet turnover and only 6 percent of their total trade with non-Communist countries. Although Soviet commercial activities have increased in Africa since that time, they still lag far behind those of the West.

[6] Alexander Dallin, "The Soviet Union: Political Activity," in *Africa and the Communist World*, Zbigniew Brzezinski, ed. (Stanford, California: Stanford University Press, 1963), p. 43.

[7] Robert A. Scalapino, "Sino-Soviet Competition in Africa," *Foreign Affairs*, Vol. 42 (July 1964), p. 649.

By the mid-1960s, it became clear that the role of irresponsible adventurer in African affairs was being played by the Red Chinese, not the Russians. Indeed, one of Europe's most respected journalists, Hugo Portisch, has noted that the Russians have not supported several Red China ploys, much to the resentment of the Chinese. Portisch, editor of Vienna's largest newspaper, *Kurier,* reported after a two-month tour of Red China:

The Chinese also hold the Soviet Union at least partly responsible for many more failures Chinese foreign policy has had to suffer in the past two years. China almost succeeded in establishing a pro-Chinese Communist rule in Zanzibar, off the east coast of Africa, and held the hope of Zanzibar's becoming China's "Cuba" in Africa. The attempt failed. The Chinese-supported rebels in the Congo were defeated. On the eve of the Chinese-inspired Afro-Asian Summit Conference in Algiers, China's friend Ben Bella was ousted in Algeria. It was this conference the Chinese wanted to use to get an overwhelming vote against the Soviet Union's claim to be an Asian power. Instead, most of the Afro-Asian nations turned their back on China, and the conference never took place. . . .

Other blows followed: China's friend in Ghana, President Nkrumah, was ousted on the day he arrived for a state visit in Peking. China's most prominent ally in East Africa, Odinga Oginga in Kenya, was chased away just a few weeks later. . . .

True, these failures are not all due alone to the Soviets. But if the Soviet Union had backed the Chinese policy many of these failures could have been avoided.

So if we assume that China's foreign policy today is based on the two principles—of national struggle aimed at regaining China's former borders, and of making China the leading power in Asia and even Africa—it is quite clear that this Chinese policy is not only challenged by the United States, but that the Soviet challenge seems of a much more lasting and deeper nature.[8]

Thus it seems self-evident that Western policy must take into consideration the difference between Soviet Russia and Communist China as competitors and tacticians in the struggle

[8] Hugo Portisch, "The Chinese-Soviet Gap Widens," *Saturday Review,* July 2, 1966.

involving the Third World. Professor Richard Lowenthal has pinpointed the underlying difference by noting that the Russians are emphasizing the class struggle while the Chinese are emphasizing "a belief in revolution at any price—even if it be a racial revolution."[9] Thus the Chinese role of unrestrained adventurer.

Because it lacks the resources for large-scale aid and because of its ideological role of revolutionary, Red China travels lightly—and often lives dangerously—in Africa. It has invaded the same socio-economic and political areas as the Russians, but its tactics can be characterized as the dangerous thrust rather than the sustained effort. The Chinese have tried to move with speed and have not hesitated to raise havoc and invite chaos.

In their economic moves, careful timing has been the keynote. When Guinea broke with France in 1958, Red China immediately shipped in two shiploads of rice. A gift of $4.7 million was made to Egypt after the Suez crisis in 1956. An offer of $75 to $150 million was made for construction of a railroad linking Ndola in Zambia with Dar es Salaam in Tanzania. In volume, the Russians provided five times the aid given by the Chinese to Africa between 1954 and 1965. In the same period, Western aid commitments were, in turn, five times that of all Communist countries. Chinese trade with Africa is even more limited: only 5 percent of China's world trade is conducted with Africa and a mere 2 percent of Africa's total trade is with Red China.

In keeping with their streamlined approach, the Chinese have tried for maximum impact with their aid by making their assistance interest-free and repayable in goods, rather than money. The technicians who accompany Chinese aid have a shirt-sleeve style and can be seen working side by side with the

[9] Richard Lowenthal, "China," in Brzezinski, *op. cit.*, p. 203.

local people and living with them as well. Although the praise heaped upon them by President Keita of Mali must be adjusted for its rhetoric, it does reflect an impression often made by the Red Chinese. Keita thanked Red China "for the reasonable cost of its technical assistance, for the ease with which its technicians adapt themselves to the life of this country, and for the competence with which it is carrying out the projects entrusted to it, and this without the least interference in our internal affairs."

The Red Chinese have backed up their campaign in Africa with a many-sided propaganda offensive using radio, print and motion pictures. One example was *Eagle in the Formosa Straits,* an English-language film casting the United States in the villain's role for its support of Chiang Kai-shek. The New China News Agency has been operating out of Cairo since 1958 and opening offices throughout the continent. For the Red Chinese version of world affairs, there is *The Peking Review,* published in English, French, Spanish and Portuguese.

In radio propaganda, Red China was in the field two years before Russia beamed broadcasts at Africa in 1958. By 1963, China's broadcast hours for Africa had grown to 70 hours weekly in a variety of languages—English, French, Portuguese, Swahili, Arabic, Hausa and, for the Chinese communities in the Malagasy Republic and southeastern Africa, Cantonese. The Chinese have, in the process, tried to pirate the prestige of the BBC by using station chimes similar to those of BBC, British-accented announcers and a frequency close to that of BBC.

In their approaches to journalists, trade unionists and students, the Chinese have demonstrated their competition with the Russians—to little avail and with scant success. The Chinese attacked the pro-Soviet leadership of the International Organization of Journalists, but failed to dislodge Russian control. A rival organization was then set up—the pro-Chinese Afro-Asian Journalists Association (AAJA). A similar tactic was tried against the Soviet-dominated WFTU in the trade-union field, also without success. The Chinese tried and failed to create their union following, but the Afro-Asian Workers Conference scheduled for October 1963 never materialized.

In the competition for African students, Moscow is far ahead of Peking, and for those Africans who have gone to Red China for study the results have been disillusioning. Their movements were restricted, living conditions uncomfortable and, worst of all for Chinese pretensions in Africa, racial discrimination was common. In 1964, Emmanuel John Hevi of Ghana, general secretary of the Union of African Students in China, published a full-scale indictment of the treatment accorded African students in China. Writing of his experience in *An African Student in China,* Hevi reports: "Out of a total of 118 African students who studied in China in my time (1961), 96 had actually left and a further 10 had signified their intention to leave by the time I had packed my bags." The repeated reasons: boredom, poor quality of instruction and, particularly, racism.

Within Africa, Red China has most strenuously acted out its adventurer's role in the explosive arena of subversion. It has been noted that "the Chinese Communists appear to be involved, directly or indirectly, in every active revolution on the African continent at present."[10] Red China has rushed to ship money and military supplies wherever they will fuel the fires of unrest and warfare. Arms were sent to the Watusis in the Burundi uprisings, to the guerrillas in Cameroon, to the Congo, to Niger.

[10] Scalapino, *op. cit.,* p. 646.

Further proof of Chinese support for subversives and guerrillas emerged after the overthrow of Nkrumah. While both Russian and Chinese technicians were involved in Ghana, the Chinese ran the guerrilla training camp known as the "Ghana Bureau of African Affairs," opened in 1963. The facts were soon publicized in a variety of publications—ranging from the *New Nigerian* to *The New York Times*. Correspondent Frank Kearns stated in a "top secret report from Ghana" over the CBS television network on June 10, 1966: "For actual guerrilla warfare, Nkrumah called in Soviet experts to set up secret camps in the bush. Later, Chinese Communists replaced the Soviets in this Chinese specialty of revolutionary war. Highly trained graduates of many nationalities are now spread all over Africa including friendly countries—so called 'freedom fighters,' trained and Communist-indoctrinated by the Red Chinese."

When we analyze the implications of Chinese tactics for Western policy, the problem of subversion becomes many-sided. The African governments are threatened at a time when the West is working for stability in the Third World. Since the local governments naturally are determined, as well, to resist subversion, they often have turned against the Red Chinese, considering them provocateurs.

President Ahidjo of Cameroon refused to recognize Communist China or support its admission to the United Nations because "China fosters the Cameroon rebellion . . . and therefore does not fulfill the fundamental conditions prescribed by the Charter." Ivory Coast President Houphouet-Boigny has said that Peking wants "to assassinate those who are aware of the Chinese peril and replace them with servile leaders who would open the gates of Africa to the Chinese." At a meeting of thirteen French-speaking nations in Nouakchott, Mauritania, in 1965, President Hamani Diori of

Niger said: "The question before us is to preserve Africa from the grip of Chinese Communists."

On the face of it, African sensitivity and strong adverse reactions to Chinese interference represent significant assets for Western policy in regard to the Third World.

An additional factor is the reaction against the Russian-Chinese competition, which is using the nations of the Third World as its battleground. Speaking as president of the All-African Trade Union Federation, Mahjoub ben Seddik told writer John K. Cooley, "We are sick and tired of the Chinese and the Russians fighting their battles among us. The only answer is a free, strong and completely independent African labor movement. Eventually, this is what we will have."[11]

Or as one Kenyan delegate summed up the African reaction at a 1964 meeting of the Afro-Asian People's Solidarity Organization:

We are not Marxist-Leninists, and most of us have never read a single line of *Das Kapital*. So what interest do you have in our participating in your doctrinal quarrels? I have had enough, when I am eating a sandwich, of being accosted by someone who asks me what I think of the Soviet positions, and when I am drinking coffee, by someone who questions me about the Chinese arguments. I would like to be able to eat in peace.

To eat in peace, to live in peace, to develop their countries in peace—that is the irresistible drive in the Third World. But as long as the Sino-Soviet bloc continues its efforts to impose its dialectical aims on developing countries this fundamental goal is endangered. In diminishing the possibility that they will fall into the Sino-Soviet sphere of influence, the developing states clearly serve their own best interests.

[11] John K. Cooley, *East Wind over Africa* (New York: Walker and Company, 1965), p. 209.

CHAPTER SIX

UNITED STATES POLICY OF

PRAGMATIC IDEALISM

Possibly more than in any other nation, the United
States foreign policy has reflected the national mood, character and code of ideals. In the ups and downs, gains and losses
of international diplomacy, America's inspired moves and self-
defeating missteps all have been connected—in one way or
another—with the American creed. Eventually, every American President and every Secretary of State has had to render
an accounting of his foreign policy in terms of the accepted
ideals of America.

Thus, the American creed is the place to begin in describing
and assessing United States policy in regard to the Third
World. Indeed, nowhere else in the world is the American
creed so applicable and so challenged to achieve its goals as in
the developing countries of Africa and Asia. This is the
ultimate context within which both the Peace Corps and
foreign military assistance are judged at home, however dis-
parate their functions.

71

From the French aristocrat Alexis de Tocqueville to the English academic D. W. Brogan and the Swedish economist Gunnar Myrdal, the American creed and character have constituted a subject of fascination to the observer from abroad. Americas, too, have added their own introspection, creating a many-sided mirror of the American way of life. It is a familiar and widely accepted rubric of traits, all of them readily translated into United States policy in the Afro-Asian world.

This was well stated by President Johnson in his message commemorating the third anniversary of the Organization of African Unity. On May 26, 1966, he told the African ambassadors:

> The foreign policy of the United States is rooted in its life at home. We will not permit human rights to be restricted in our own country. And we will not support policies abroad which are based on the rule of minorities or the discredited notion that men are unequal before the law.
> We will not live by a double standard—professing abroad what we do not practice at home, or venerating at home what we ignore abroad.[1]

Americans, with their celebration of the wisdom and the dignity of the common man, are committed to the equality of all men—even when they do not practice what they preach. Idealistic, but also pragmatic, Americans are more concerned with making things work than with working out ideas. When Americans espouse democracy it is less in a rigid, doctrinaire fashion than in a frame of mind which guarantees individual freedom. From this stems America's concern for racial and religious tolerance and its rejection of class and caste. The American creed is idealistic, pragmatic and egalitarian and these same ingredients permeate American foreign policy with

[1] Text in *The New York Times,* May 27, 1966.

the Third World—in spite of contradictions, evasions and inconsistencies.

United States policy has a minimum practical goal rooted in the nation's role as the major Western power: to prevent the Afro-Asian world from falling into the Communist sphere of influence. The United States seeks to develop a reserve of friendly relationships and a basis for mutually meaningful cooperation.

Generally, American policy crystallized slowly. As a Western power, an overriding goal for the United States was maintenance of satisfactory relations with the major powers of Western Europe—who were also the colonial powers in Africa and Asia. While the United States in the late 1940s and early 1950s encouraged England, France and the Netherlands to accept the inevitability of independence for their Asian colonies, it was general policy to allow the European governments to take the lead in these changes. Needless to say, as the source of the Marshall Plan aid in Europe, the United States was in a favorable power position to influence the European powers in this regard.

In Africa—first in North Africa with Libyan independence in 1949 and then beginning in Black Africa in 1957 with the Gold Coast's independence—the United States openly encouraged a rapid transfer of power to the local peoples. The position of the United States was known to all those active on the scene, and a good number of African nationalists received spiritual as well as material support from the United States. While the European powers had to take the formal steps in the process of change, the United States posture was thoroughly in keeping with the American creed.

With the spread of independence, the new countries strove to develop foreign policies, giving rise to the position of non-alignment. This, is turn, led to the "alignment of the non-aligned," dramatized by the Bandung Conference of 1955 and underlined by the Belgrade Conference of 1961. For the first time in its peacetime history the United States faced a significant configuration of power that was non-white. To protect its own interests, the United States chose a variety of responses— from the minimum of preventing Communist take-overs to the maximum of close alliances.

While encouraging the transfer of power to the Afro-Asian peoples, the United States launched technical-assistance and cultural-exchange programs. Both activities had a clear motive: the development of national economies as the most promising basis for friendly relations with the new Afro-Asian states. The relative scale of United States aid to the Afro-Asian countries in comparison to aid from China and the Soviet Union can be seen in Table 1.

Thus in the post-World War II period, the United States policy of favoring independence was translated into economic support for the emerging countries. But a negative note was also present; the anti-colonialism of the United States evolved under Secretary of State John Foster Dulles into anti-neutralism. In the Dulles view, nations were either *for* or *against* us. In 1956, he described neutralism as the principle "which pretends that a nation can best gain safety for itself by being indifferent to the fate of others." In the Afro-Asian world, the United States sought allies as it did in Western Europe under a simplified division of leaders and power elements according to their allegiance in the East-West struggle.

If the 1950s was the decade of asking the Third World nations to take sides, the 1960s was the decade of accepting real neutralism, and of pinning American policy on the dynamic urge for independence. President Kennedy personified the shift in United States policy, for he built America's hopes in the Third World on the nation's "magic power." In 1959,

TABLE 1.   UNITED STATES, CHINA AND USSR
ECONOMIC AID COMMITMENTS, 1946–1966[a]
(in millions of dollars)

	UNITED STATES		CHINA	USSR	
	Total	Including Food for Peace		Loans	Grants
Afghanistan	271	62	28	377	150
Algeria	150	146	55–60	228	
Argentina	653	18	—	100	
Burma	110	49	84–88	10–15	
Cambodia	261	2	55–60	12	6
Ceylon	87	65	31–41	30	
Congo-Brazzaville	5	—	25	9	
Ethiopia	130	15	—	100	2
Ghana	163	6	42	82	
Guinea	47	19	32	61–85	
India	5,192	2,369	—	806[b]	
Indonesia	831	315	100–108	367–375	
Iran	798	96	—	39	
Iraq	47	19	—	183	
Kenya	26	10	18–28	3	
Laos	417	—	?	4	
Mali	12	—	20	61	
Morocco	451	179	—	?	
Nepal	72	37	43–71	3	11
Pakistan	2,631	959	90	80–100	
Senegal	15	5	—	7	
Somali	39	4	23	52	
Sudan	81	13	—	22	
Syria	82	62	16–20	87	
Tanzania	38	16	43	42	
Tunisia	396	180	—	29	
Turkey	1,933	385	—	168–178	
UAR	943	715	85	821	
Uganda	15	1	15	16	
Yemen	35	10	44–49	92	
Zambia	—	—	0.5	—	
TOTAL	15,931	5,757	849–929	3,891–3,958	169

[a] Figures for United States to mid-1964; for China and USSR to mid-1966.
[b] Plus a reported $800 to be given during the fourth five-year plan.
Source: Current History, August 1966, p. 80.

he told James MacGregor Burns: "The 'magic power' on our side is the desire of every person to be free, of every nation to be independent. . . . It is because I believe our system is more in keeping with the fundamentals of human nature that I believe we are ultimately going to be successful."[2]

The United States acceptance of neutralism in the Third World has been particularly evident in its dealings with India and Pakistan. India receives most of its military equipment from the Soviet Union and its food from the United States. In other words, the Indian armed forces are equipped by Moscow but fed by Washington. Pakistan is on excellent terms with Communist China, and yet the West sends her massive military aid. In these two cases, the United States does not inflict the penalties of neutrality upon these countries. Instead, she accepts their stance and derives the best possible benefit from it.

It is within this context that the United States faces its most disturbing foreign challenge of the 1960s in regard to the Third World. That challenge—arising from a racial confrontation—is southern Africa, where an intransigent white minority is fighting against independence for the black majority. It is also that part of Africa which represents an economic prize.

While Vietnam has become an issue of major concern to the West, the war there represents only a manifestation of the problem of the revolution of color rather than the problem as such. By fighting to protect this Asian country against Communism, the United States is seen in the Third World as pursuing the ideological battle of the Cold War. By and large, the Afro-Asian states do not respond to the Vietnam question in terms of the East-West struggle for supremacy. Instead, they view it in terms of Western intrusion and intrigue. One

[2] Quoted by Arthur M. Schlesinger, Jr., in *A Thousand Days* (Boston: Houghton Mifflin Co., 1965), p. 508.

might dismiss their opinions as mistaken and even cranky. To its credit, Washington has not done so, and the unending efforts of Ambassador-at-Large Averell Harriman and other emissaries have been aimed at explaining United States policy.

In the case of southern Africa, the Western presence in a Third-World country is militant, mercenary, repressive and racist. With favorable climate, fertile soil and natural resources, southern Africa looms large and ominous. There are the countries of Portuguese domination, Angola and Mozambique; South-West Africa, which is under South African government control; the Republic of South Africa; and Rhodesia, which boldly challenged the principle of majority rule with its 1965 Unilateral Declaration of Independence. While Angola and Mozambique are ruled as provinces of Portugal, the other areas are under local control.

The repressive colonial policy of Portugal (discussed in Chapter Seven) poses a strategic problem to the United States since Portugal is a member of the North Atlantic Treaty Organization and long-time ally of Western powers. Portugal not only has refused to accept the thesis enunciated by Western political and religious leaders on the right of self-determination, but has launched a sustained military effort to destroy the movements encouraging independence. While the United Kingdom and France welcomed the Afro-Asian leaders to negotiate the time and circumstances of independence, the Portuguese have declared that nationalist leaders in their territories are traitors.

As a result, the intransigence of the Portuguese has been harmful to the United States relations with the Third World. Various Afro-Asian powers have charged that the United States, as the major Western power, has not done enough to influence its Portuguese ally to change position and follow the course of other European governments. In the final analysis, the Third World will be satisfied only when the peoples in the Portuguese colonies can exercise their right of self-determination.

Much more harmful to United States relations with Afro-Asian countries is the situation in the white minority–dominated areas of the Republic of South Africa, South-West Africa and Rhodesia. There, peoples of color are forcibly confined to an inferior position for the benefit of the white minority. Nowhere is the horror of white domination over non-white more apparent, more determined and more explosive. The dread word, *apartheid* for apartness, has been properly characterized by novelist Alan Paton as "the finest blend of cruelty and idealism ever devised by man." The idealism is perverted, the cruelty oppressive.

For a nation like the United States, which became history's haven for the oppressed, South Africa is a cold-blooded mockery of the American creed. In South Africa, oppression wears the mantle of legality in which a monstrous, perverted Judgment Angel has decided who shall live like a human being and who shall not, who shall be white and favored, and who shall not. The language of racial definition in South Africa seems to deny the subject being defined: a human being. A native is a person "who in fact is or is generally accepted as a member of any aboriginal race or tribe of Africa." A white person is one who "in appearance obviously is or who is generally accepted as a white person, but does not include a person who, although in appearance obviously is a white person, is generally accepted as a colored person."

When the apartheid policy was ruthlessly intensified in 1948, probably the most bizarre governmental proceedings in modern history took place. In towns throughout South Africa, boards met to decide on the status of dark whites and light Negroes. In the same family, one brother was declared white and the others Negro. The satanic process of designation determined whether the victims would be bound in the chains of South African race laws.

The Orwellian legal litany includes the Prohibition of Mixed Marriages Act, the Immorality Amendment Act, the Separate Representation of Voters Act, the Bantu Authorities Act, the Group Areas Acts, the Reservation of Separate Amenities Act, the Native Labor Act, the Suppression of Communism Act, the Church Clause, the Twelve-Day Detention Clause, the 90-Day Detention Clause and the 180-Day Detention Clause.

For the South African non-white, life is lived by the book— the passbook. It contains the infamous stamps which *permit* him to look for a job, hold a job, live in his residence, even live with his own wife and children. He needs a special stamp permitting him to get on a train and he can lose any and all of these stamps at the whim of the government.

For the South African non-white, life is also lived *apart* from white trains, buses, taxis, public restrooms, churches, schools. He cannot even sit on park benches marked for whites only. He may use the same postage stamps as whites, but he must enter the post office through a separate door and buy the stamps at a separate window.

By a grisly extension of repression, the whites in South Africa feels the overflow of the system, since injustice eventually penalizes both the oppressor and the oppressed. Anyone in South Africa can be held in jail for 180 days—without charge. Anyone considered too critical of the regime can be confined to his home for years. It is hardly a surprise that this system developed under the direction of the then Justice Minister Johannes Balthazar Vorster, who once spent two years in a South African internment camp for pro-Nazi activities. Following the assassination of Dr. Verwoerd, he was named Prime Minister.

The perverted determination of 3.5 million whites to dominate a South African population of 18.3 million reverberated to the north in Rhodesia, where a 5-percent minority of whites assumed the role of dominating the overwhelming black majority. It also continued defiantly in the mandated territory of South-West Africa, where South Africa won a victory in July 1966, when the Court of International Justice did not hold the Republic in violation of its 46-year-old League of Nations mandate. The Court actually avoided making a decision on the merits of the case.

This represented a disappointing setback for the Afro-Asian world, which had planned a major assault in the United Nations upon South African policies. If the Court had condemned the Republic and the decision were flouted, the Afro-Asian countries would probably have succeeded in obtaining a General Assembly recommendation for Security Council action in South-West Africa. Instead, there were celebrations in South Africa, where special thanksgiving services were held.

There was also disappointment in the United States, which had taken a strong stand for adherence to the Court decision—which had been expected to be against South Africa. The Republic had already rejected the United States contention that the Court's earlier advisory opinions had confirmed the validity of the mandate and required South Africa to accept United Nations supervision.

As the southern Africa crisis mounted in the 1950s and 1960s, the United States took increasing cognizance of its responsibilities in that area. An emphatic demonstration of the United States attitude was evident on May 26, 1966, when President Johnson depicted the racial doctrines of Rhodesia and South Africa as repulsive. It was tantamount to accepting the Afro-Asian contention that the racial policies of South Africa and Rhodesia are a matter of international concern and responsibility.

In this regard, the visit of Senator Robert F. Kennedy to South Africa in June 1966 was carefully watched by Third World leaders and the university students who will provide the next generation of leaders. Senator Kennedy branded apartheid as one of the evils of the world, in a major address to the National Union of South African Students at the University of Capetown. The younger brother of the late President Kennedy made an impassioned plea for an end to societies based on racial differences, and he did not spare his own country. He stressed that the United States has "many long miles" to go in trying to implement full brotherhood. His appeal to white South Africans was unequivocal: join the forward march of the rest of the Western world, which is trying to end separation and prejudice.

But the Kennedy and Johnson pronouncements still do not satisfy Afro-Asian demands for direct follow-up action. In the same year that these two impeccable statements of American policy and attitude were made by these men, the forces advocating racism in South Africa, Rhodesia and South-West Africa consolidated their positions. In order to comprehend the overpowering reactions in the Third World toward racial problems in southern Africa, it is necessary to realize that the doctrine of apartheid humiliates all men of color and elicits a complex of negative responses. The man of color cannot be half-hearted on this issue. It is asking Jews to "understand" Hitler.

Still, why do members of the Third World hold the South African situation against the United States? As the major power in the Western world, the United States is clearly expected by the Third World to remedy the gross evil of apartheid in southern Africa by initiating a series of actions designed to bring about peaceful internal change. The United States is also expected to dramatize its disapproval of the treatment of Africans by the South African government as it has dramatized its disapproval of Hitler's treatment of the Jews and the Russian treatment of Eastern Europeans. When this is not done, the Afro-Asian community naturally suspects that it may be because those suffering in this instance are non-whites.

Despite its good intentions, the United States is severely criticized. Indeed, there would seem to be in the Third World a layer of latent anti-Americanism. This sometimes spurts to the surface when events like the Belgian-American intervention in the Congo take place. What is responsible for this? The best seller, *The Ugly American,* suggested outright bungling, and no doubt some of this occurs.

But there seems to be a more fundamental reason. The price the U.S. seems fated to pay for overwhelming power is unpopularity. (Incidentally, the Soviets have the same difficulty.) American might overawes the Afro-Asians. It is all-pervasive, it is lopsided. That is to say that the United States is always giving and the Third World is always receiving. It can never reciprocate in kind, but it can form a partnership for progress—a partnership that benefits the entire world, rich and poor.

The appropriate response of the West—as verbalized in Capetown by Senator Kennedy—is to combat injustice every-where, to recognize that a single bell tolls for the entire world, to proclaim the global dimensions of the fight for human dignity. Senator Kennedy's statement was particularly effec-tive in addressing the emerging generation of all nations:

Each nation has different obstacles and different goals, shaped by the vagaries of history and experience. Yet as I talk to young people around the world I am impressed not by diversity but by the closeness of their goals, their desires and concerns and hope for the future. There is discrimination in New York, apartheid in

South Africa and serfdom in the mountains of Peru. People starve in the streets in India; intellectuals go to jail in Russia; thousands are slaughtered in Indonesia; wealth is lavished on armaments everywhere. These are differing evils. But they are the common works of man.

And therefore they call upon common qualities of conscience and of indignation, a shared determination to wipe away the unnecessary sufferings of our fellow human beings at home and particularly around the world.

The link between American race relations at home and foreign policy toward the Third World is direct and crucial. Slightly more than one in ten Americans is a Negro, representing both challenge and opportunity to the United States at home and abroad. The United States Constitution, coupled with recent legislation and Supreme Court decisions, provides the backdrop for turning the United States into a showcase of racial harmony. Many other nations have a similar framework of constitutional and legal protection against racial discrimination, but the United States is the only Western country with a significant number of non-whites to demonstrate racial pluralism on a wide scale.

The sudden shrinking of time and distance have placed the peoples of the Third World in the same global village with the American people. They now observe at first hand what the United States is doing to integrate its society fully. Only a fast-moving, all-inclusive campaign to eliminate the vestiges of second-class status will have any substantial appeal to the Third World. For the first time in its history, the United States is faced with the fact that an urgent domestic matter vitally affects its foreign policy. The ability of the United States to maintain friendly relations abroad with the Afro-Asian community will be directly affected by the civil rights story at home.

The concern of Americans in regard to their race problem

is reflected in the continuous charting of progress and, also, of the setbacks in realizing full equality. One of the most influential and widely read examples of stock-taking was the mid-summer 1966 survey published by *Newsweek* magazine.[3] Comparing the findings with an earlier survey in 1963, the results constituted an "encouraging picture of progress." The survey of Negroes found:

—54 percent had more job satisfaction than in 1963, whereas 45 percent noted such improvement in 1963.

—55 percent found it easier to eat in restaurants, whereas 36 percent noted improvements in 1963.

—58 percent felt they were better off in regard to integrated schooling compared with 39 percent registering improvement in 1963.

—53 percent cited improvements in registration and voting compared with 31 percent in 1963.

For 21 million Negro Americans, there was a feeling that progress is continuing. Two out of three Negroes in the survey felt that things in general were better in 1966 than in 1963. Change was felt most forcibly in the South, where three out of four Negroes noted improvements in their way of life, but of course in the South the starting point left a much greater distance to travel toward Negro equality. But the lesson and the outcome no longer hinge on whether America is moving in the right direction. Except for extremists of the right and the left and extremists among whites and non-whites, Americans agree that the country is on the move in solving its civil rights problems.

But is that movement fast enough? The 1966 outbreaks in the North showed that much remains to be done to achieve racial harmony. The lower the whites on the American social

---

[3] *Newsweek*, August 22, 1966.

ladder, the more resistant they are to civil rights progress, and it is here that American leadership faces a severe challenge. Most of all, there is the crisis of the American city and the cancerous black ghettos that are permitted to spread in the heart of metropolitan areas. Referring to 1966, Martin Luther King said: "The most significant event of the year is the spread of the Negro Revolution from the sprawling plantations of Mississippi and Alabama to the desolate slums and ghettos of the North."

In outlining the "redirection of American power" toward solution of the civil rights problem, Dr. Kenneth B. Clark, one of the most perceptive experts working in this area, has discussed the triggering forces at work in the national commitment to racial harmony. He cites the ideological, psychological and military competition that subjects American ideals —and their non-observance—to new challenges. He also points out the role of rising nationalism in Asia and Africa: "The whole world, in fact, has been undergoing a racial revolution, a breakdown in imperialism and a change in the relationship between white Europeans and colored peoples. White and Negro Americans could not escape the impact of this world-wide racial revolution."[4]

United States policy toward the Afro-Asian world soon recognized the power of nationalism and the same obsession for self-rule that is felt in Europe and North America. Starting first in Asia, then continuing in Africa, the United States encouraged the European powers to accelerate the process of decolonialization. Simultaneously the United States initiated cultural exchange and technical assistance programs with the new nations. But not until the 1960s did the United States

[4] Kenneth B. Clark, "The Dilemma of Power," in *The Negro American,* edited by Talcott Parsons and Kenneth B. Clark (Boston: Houghton Mifflin Co., 1966), pp. xiv–xv.

fully take into account the important of the race factor that is present in all aspects of its relationships with the Third World.

In the latter half of the 1960s, the United States policy toward the Third World was confronted by one overpowering challenge abroad and one at home—each representing a fundamental confrontation with the American creed and its emphasis on equality. In facing the challenge at home, the United States was clearly moving toward the creation of a showcase for racial harmony. Only the tempo was at issue, not the direction. In facing racial oppression in southern Africa, the United States policy was clearer than its actions. In both instances, there was acceptance in official government circles and among intellectuals, leaders and opinion makers that the future of United States policy with the Third World depended largely on the racial issue. In this regard, if the historical trend continues, United States policy would once again prove itself consistent with the American creed.

CHAPTER SEVEN

THE ROLE OF

WESTERN EUROPE

The adjustment of Western Europe to the post-World War II emergence of the Third World has involved a workable combination of pragmatism, self-interest, ideology and culture. Only Portugal persists in its refusal to adjust to the realities of the situation.

In fact, intellectual and cultural institutions in Europe came to terms with the significance of the Third World and its impact on international affairs before American institutions did. Nonetheless, the Third World's social and cultural impact on both Western Europe and the United States is just beginning. In the end, the adjustment of the Western world to the decline of the white Anglo-Saxon Protestant ethic and to pressures on the Western values may be more drastic than the adjustment required by the decline of white political power in world affairs.

Following World War II, France, the United Kingdom, the Netherlands and Belgium recognized the significance of the

87

decline of absolute Western power and the inevitability of the rise to power of the Afro-Asian peoples. They realized that it was in their best interest to cooperate with this inevitability. They cooperated in various ways and at different tempos but with a common hope that their economic and socio-cultural interests could be salvaged.

In retrospect, we can see that British and French colonialism had set the stage for independence. They not only introduced concepts of colonial administration, but also instilled certain philosophical views that were the products of their own histories. Because educational curriculums in the colonial areas emphasized European history and institutions, Afro-Asian students read of the French Revolution and British constitutional history. They encountered a series of "dangerous ideas": that every man has the right to revolt against a tyranny, that the people have the right to participate in the institutions governing them, that government must exist for the good of all people and not for the few, that there were inalienable human rights, that since all men were equal the same opportunities should be available equally to all. To these ideas, imbedded in European tradition, were added the socialist theories of revolutionary action to correct the social evils of economic exploitation.

These ideas gained momentum in Africa and Asia at a time when colonial power was declining and the idea of self-determination was gaining acceptance throughout Europe. Europe was confronted with the dilemma of having fought two world wars for freedom and democracy while holding back from applying these same principles to the colonial peoples in Africa and Asia. Moreover, World War II had left Europe prostrate as the result of the tremendous human and material toll. All available energy was needed to reconstruct a new life out of the damage and chaos. Europe had neither the resources nor the will to perpetuate the old colonial system. Meanwhile, pressure was applied by the United States, whose traditional anti-colonial policies were often at variance with the policies of her allies.

Self-determination still had to be expressed in timetables, constitutional revisions and social and economic adjustments, and the United Nations became the main forum for airing disagreements during the transitional period. While the Trusteeship Council had jurisdiction over only a small portion of the non-self-governing territories, it did afford the international community with a means of checking the administration of the trusteeship mandate and debating each territory's progress toward self-determination. For added pressure, there was the anti-colonial posture of the Soviet Union.

When the French flag came down in favor of the flags of fourteen different African states, a chapter had closed on an empire that had reached its peak at the end of World War I. The French view of self-government involved a unity between the dependency and the metropolis. A process of colonization, which had begun in the fourteenth century, culminated in a community of French-speaking nations established in the middle of the twentieth century. The colonial policy of assimilation became translated into close economic, cultural and social links with Paris.

The postwar evolution of French policy process could be traced from the participation of overseas representatives in drafting the 1946 French Constitution. The Brazzaville Conference of 1944 had already modified the concept of assimilation and unity to mean "federation"—increased responsibility at the local level with control still at the center. By 1956, assimilation as a desirable and achievable goal had been abandoned altogether and the French government accepted the idea of internal autonomy. With the coming of the Fifth

Republic in 1958, overseas territories were given six months to choose whether to retain their status, become an overseas department more closely integrated with the Republic or become an autonomous state within the newly formed French Community. Only Guinea voted—on September 28, 1958—for immediate independence outside the Community. In June 1960 the constitution was amended to enable sovereign member states to remain within the Community. A commonwealth was, in effect, created.

By the early 1960s, France was concentrating on cultural and economic ties with her former territories as political relations became those of sovereign states. The French colonist was withdrawing in favor of the French schoolteacher, trader and banker, but the intense sphere of French interest remained. The Quai d'Orsay zealously guarded French prerogatives, and a no-trespassing sign was often encountered by nations on either side of the Iron Curtain. In her former colonies, France remained a strong presence—often a prompter—in the wings.

Next, France disassociated herself from many aspects of Anglo-American policies and was projecting, by the mid-1960s, an independent role with the Third World. A major difference of opinion developed over Vietnam, which France had lost in the mid-1950s. The French protectorate over Vietnam, which had begun in 1884, ended in May 1954 at the Battle of Dienbienphu—a death blow to any dreams of empire. In effect, France was trying to re-enter the Asian scene via the back door.

President de Gaulle made this attempt at re-entry with his characteristic flair. On January 27, 1964, he stunned the world by announcing the establishment of diplomatic relations between France and Red China. He did not consult his Western allies about the wisdom of this move. But this very act

endeared him to the Third World, for it showed his independence of Washington. Now there is a booming trade going on.
To understand President de Gaulle's designs on the Afro-
Asian world, one must see them in terms of his larger aim of
bringing grandeur to France. His Asian moves then consist in
strengthening French ties with India and Japan, for these are
potentially powerful states, worthy of respect even now. For
the former French Indochina, he advocates full independence
—an aim which is naturally hailed by the Afro-Asians while it
embarrasses some of his Western allies. In explosive Southeast
Asia, he favors neutrality with the consquent termination of
the SEATO alliance. The non-aligned, even Ho Chi Minh,
rejoice at this line since it agrees, or so they say, with their
own inclinations. All these actions create goodwill for France
and respect for her independence of view. For the West,
especially for Washington, they create embarrassment.

In the process of disengaging herself from NATO, France
simultaneously sought a leadership role vis-à-vis the Third
World. General de Gaulle extended this campaign to Latin
America in 1965 pointing out the common denominator of
Latin culture between the French and South American states.
However, France's former major colonial role, coupled with
her major power position in the West, handicapped her
campaign for leadership in her relations with the Third World.

After World War II, British policy toward the Afro-Asian
world entered the third and final colonial phase. Independence
came soon after. The first stage had been a laissez-faire
attitude based on expansion of British commercial interests;
next came the extension of imperial power and introduction of
indirect rule. The final postwar phase stressed promotion of
economic and social development as the essential base for self-
government.

The British postwar pattern of independence began in Asia

and was dramatized by the emergence of India and Pakistan in 1947. Ten years later, the pattern was extended to Africa when independence was granted to the Gold Coast, which became Ghana. The orderly transfer of power from British hands to the local peoples continued at rapid pace in Africa. In 1946, Northern Rhodesia and Nyasaland became independent and took the names of Zambia and Malawi.

The rapport of the British government with the Third World was made closer by the presence of Afro-Asian members in the Commonwealth. However, the Unilateral Declaration of Independence in Southern Rhodesia in 1965 by a white supremist minority and Britain's hesitant response clouded her relationship with the Afro-Asian powers. The Southern Rhodesia action struck at the heart of Afro-Asian sensitivity—racism. Afro-Asians regard Southern Rhodesian illegal independence action as a bare-faced attempt to turn Rhodesia into an independent apartheid-oriented state like the Republic of South Africa. Third-World nations demanded that Britain assert her legal control over Rhodesia to protect the interests of the black majority.

In breaking diplomatic relations with the United Kingdom on this issue, Tanzania's President Nyerere reflected the views of the Third World:

It is vital that Africa's legitimate concern in this matter should be recognized. For each African nation has had to overcome the power of racialism in order to become independent. It is, to us, the ultimate horror. We can never surrender to it, or allow it to continue unchallenged on the African continent. Our own future is too much involved.[1]

Afro-Asian reaction to the United Kingdom was influenced by the British attitude on race. While official policies preach

[1] Julius K. Nyerere, "Rhodesia in the Context of Southern Africa," *Foreign Affairs*, April 1966, p. 386.

full equality for all regardless of race, there is inherent in the Western milieu an implicit attitude of superiority resulting from centuries of dominance. Afro-Asians, naturally, resent this wherever it appears. In the Rhodesia issue, this factor jeopardized rapport between the United Kingdom and the Third World.

There remain, however, the factors of language and similar governmental and educational institutions which form the basis for dialogue between the United Kingdom and her former colonies in the Third World. Along with economic assistance from England, this can help balance, in the long run, the resentment felt on the Rhodesian and race issues.

Indeed, the record of the United Kingdom in her former colonial territories in Africa and Asia augurs well for the future. After granting independence she has at their own request borne the burden of Commonwealth aid to these areas. In keeping with the proposals of the 1958 Common-wealth Trade and Economic Conference, she contributed 100 million pounds a year. In this work private investment does not lag far behind. According to the 1959–60 *Survey of International Affairs* (an annual publication of the Royal Institute of International Affairs of London), British invest-ment in India by the end of 1959 constituted 81 percent of all foreign investments there.[2]

Furthermore, despite talk of reducing defense commitments "east of Suez," Britain helps Malaysia and Singapore in bol-stering their defense against subversion.

In short, Britain lost an empire but gained immeasurable goodwill, apart from increased trade. Now she derives benefits without the odium of colonialism.

In contrast with Britain and France, which had major

[2] *Survey of International Affairs, 1959–60* (London: Oxford University Press, 1964), p. 330.

colonial holdings in Africa and Asia, Belgium and the Netherlands played restricted roles and have no major power aspirations. Nonetheless, both the Netherlands and Belgium had
turbulent post-independence relationships with their former
colonies, Indonesia and the Congo, respectively.

In the case of Belgium, these difficulties have tended to
hamper her ability to carry on meaningful dialogue with the
Third World, especially Africa. But the Netherlands, despite
difficulties with Indonesia over New Guinea, has been able to
establish close rapport with a number of Afro-Asian states. As
the influence of President Sukarno faded away and the Indonesian economy tottered, she succeeded in improving relations
with the country's new leaders by offering economic assistance.
To the West Cameroons and Brazil she sent her version of the
Peace Corps. The resolution of these difficulties has been
marked by an increase in the number of Afro-Asian students
at Dutch institutions. In The Hague, Delft, Deventer they attend practical courses in English. The fields of study range
from agriculture to hydraulic engineering.

It remains for Portugal to stand out as Europe's standard
bearer of colonial intransigence. Still a colonial power in Africa
and Asia, Portugal is unable to carry on any meaningful
contacts with the Afro-Asian world. The Portuguese insistence
on their right to rule in Africa and Asia defies not only the
Afro-Asians but also the self-determination policy practiced
by the other Western colonial powers.

Regarding her possessions in Asia and Africa, Lisbon takes
the view that they are integral parts of metropolitan Portugal.
This came out clearly in a government statement on India's
claims to Goa. "If the question of Goa is understood as a
transfer to the Indian Union of the sovereignty of Portuguese
territories, it is certain that the question will not be solved by
peaceful means."[3] But amid Western disapproval, Nehru

[3] *The Times* (London), July 23, 1955.

annexed Goa with force of arms in December 1961. One reason for this move was that for the nonaligned Indians, Portuguese presence meant, rightly or wrongly, NATO presence.

But Portugal's attitude to Timor, an island in the Indonesian archipelago, and Macao, a piece of land bordering on Red China, is less aggressive and provocative than her attitude toward her possessions in Africa. In Timor, she has haughtily ignored the occasional claim by Indonesia. As regards Macao, however, she has walked very gingerly. Though not diplomatically represented in the Communist countries because of her principled opposition to Communism, she tried to preserve good relations with Peking and to refuse to let Macao be used by elements hostile to China.

As *The New York Times* of December 28, 1966, pointed out, Macao is of historical and psychological importance to Portugal. As a part of the Portuguese empire since 1557, Macao's loss now that Portugal is fighting to retain her territories in Africa "could deal a sharp blow to the national will to resist further disintegration of the empire."

In Africa, where its major colonial holdings are still located, Portugal's policy has had two major characteristics: political unity and the substitution of Portuguese culture for African culture. As justification, the Portuguese point to the legal concept of "overseas provinces" and the cultural concept of "assimilados." Whether or not these concepts are in fact realities is the major consideration in understanding current events in Portuguese Africa.

In 1951 Portuguese law changed the designation of colonies to that of overseas provinces under the jurisdiction of the Council of Ministers as the policy-making body. Administrative problems are handled by the Minister of Overseas Provinces, who can also legislate by decree. Angola and Mozambique are directly administered by Governors-General assisted by advisory councils, which de facto ignore the interests of the more than nine million Africans in these provinces.

In refusing to grant rights to Africans, the Portuguese argued that good citizenship can only be instilled by the acceptance of their cultural values. In their view, to grant all rights based on the Portuguese constitution to "uncivilized" persons would court the abuse of these rights. Therefore, full citizenship rights were granted only to "assimilados."

By law an African could become an "assimilado" and so a citizen, if he were over eighteen years of age, spoke Portuguese satisfactorily, earned sufficient income to support himself and his family, was of good character and showed evidence of not avoiding military service. Persons fulfilling these qualifications could apply for consideration before the local authorities. Other Africans were automatically considered "assimilados" if they had performed some public service, were employed in the civil service, had acquired a secondary education or were a partner in a business. About 70,000 persons were classified as assimilados, but in recent years fewer and fewer qualified persons have even attempted to apply for consideration. But even assimilados are not, in fact, accorded equal status, Africans add.

Of reforms announced in September 1961, the United Nations committee investigating the disturbance in Angola concluded that "the recent reforms would seem to have been designed mainly as indicated by Portuguese officials, to offset alleged misunderstandings abroad and to rationalize procedures. Their immediate effect on ameliorating the conditions in the territory as recommended by the United Nations organization appears to be limited."[4]

[4] Report of the Sub-Committee on the Situation in Angola, Sixteenth Session, Agenda Item 27, United Nations General Assembly, November 22, 1961, p. 138.

Yet the Portuguese continue in their cruel fiction of equality while carrying on the fact of political control. Since 1961, the Africans have responded in Portuguese areas by struggling to spread the fires of nationalism that burn throughout Africa. Disturbances have raged in Portuguese Guinea, Angola and Mozambique. In late 1963, when representatives of 32 African states met with Portuguese representatives at the United Nations, the fundamental disagreement on self-determination was pinpointed. The Portuguese said that it meant participation in administration and public life. The Africans insisted that it should include the right to determine the territories' future.[5] Such a fundamental difference leaves the chasm between Portugal and the Third World deep, wide and dangerous.

While the Spanish flag still flies in Africa, the head of the United Nations anti-colonial committee hailed Spain in May 1966 for its policies in Africa, where it still has several territories. Spain's "bridge concept" governing relations with the North African countries has been extended to Black Africa. Her reorientation of policy became pronounced in the 1960s as Spain sought to break out of her political and economic isolation. As a consequence, in the last few years Spanish policy has exhibited a new flexibility and pragmatism in several spheres. Determined to play a significant role in international affairs, Spain is turning her attention to several major world problems, including colonialism. In an almost complete reversal of former policy, Spain is now creating a new anti-imperialist image in the Afro-Asian world.

This represents a decisive change in thinking for a nation long associated with colonialism. During Spain's golden era in the sixteenth century, the Spanish flag had flown in many parts of the New World, Asia and Africa. The prestige and glory of

[5] *The New York Times,* November 7, 1963.

her vast empire, with its cultural and religious overtones, permeated Spain's history and imbued her citizens with a pride in the past. However, after the long years of civil war and World War II, Spain was weak, ignored and isolated.

The Spanish possessions in Africa, relatively few in number and small in area, have shared in the cycle of changes in the Spanish atmosphere. Immediately after World War II, Spain tightened her colonial controls in a reaction against her European neighbors and their continued exclusiveness. It was as if she were trying desperately to hold onto the last of her glories. However, in 1962 Spain ceased looking on her colonies as "overseas provinces," a policy that she shared with her neighbor, Portugal. Instead, Spain entered a phase of reassessment during which she adjusted to the new and revolutionary changes in Africa.

Spain's holdings in Africa are divided into three categories. First, there are the "places of sovereignty" which are located in northern Morocco and consist of two towns, Ceuta and Melilla, each with about 80,000 inhabitants. Spanish occupation and possession of these towns date back to the fifteenth or sixteenth century. Physically, they exist as garrison towns for Spain's southern frontier and are regarded as part of metropolitan Spain. In population they are overwhelmingly Spanish Catholic, and although Morocco claims possession, a referendum would certainly confirm loyalty to Spain.

Ceuta has a special significance for Franco's Spain, since it was from this garrison town that the Generalissimo launched his attack upon the Republic in 1936. As mark of gratitude for the part played by Moorish contingents, Franco retained a bodyguard of Moors for the next twenty years—until Morocco's independence from France in 1956. At that time, Spain yielded her authority over the northern and southern border strips, retaining only her "places of sovereignty" and Ifni on the west coast.

Along with Spanish Sahara, Ifni represents the second category of Spanish possessions in Africa. Less than six hundred square miles in area, Ifni is completely surrounded by Morocco. Although claimed by Spain in the nineteenth century, Ifni was not occupied until 1934. The other province, Spanish Sahara, is a sandy strip of desert on the west coast of Africa between Morocco and Mauritania. Spanish rule cannot be classified as colonialism in either of these areas, since there are few settlers and they are controlled by a few military authorities. Both areas are poor, although the Sahara gives evidence of mineral wealth. The population is sparse and nomadic and there has been no attempt to assimilate these people into European culture.

The third category of Spanish possessions includes Spanish Equatorial Guinea, which is situated in Black Africa. Spanish Guinea consists of the islands of Fernando Po and a small area of the mainland, Rio Muni, bordered by Cameroons and Gabon. Despite its small size, Spanish Guinea's exports are considerable. It is in Spanish Guinea, with its population of about 250,000, that the evolution of Spain's policy can best be studied.

Spain points with pride to the health and educational facilities provided in Guinea. The government claims that 90 percent of the school-age children attend classes. Spanish paternalism even reached the point where expenditure per capita was sometimes greater than in metropolitan Spain. But it was paternalism. The schools emphasized everything Hispanic: language, culture, Church and love for Mother Spain. Those Guineans who reached a stage where they were considered evolved or civilized were assimilated into Spanish culture as "emancipados" and enjoyed the full rights and privileges of Spanish citizens. But this group was infinitesimal in number, and the majority of the non-emancipated were considered minors and had few rights under law.

In 1958, when liberation movements began to stir in Africa, Spain adopted a set of reforms that were aimed at tightening Guinea's ties with the mother country. Ifni and Spanish Sahara were officially made provinces of Spain, and in 1959 Spanish Guinea was placed in the same status. The former system of assimilation was abolished, and Spanish citizenship was granted to all inhabitants. Elections were held in 1960 and three African representatives were chosen to sit in the Spanish Cortes. Thus Spain hoped to make all her former colonies and protectorates one with the Spanish mainland.

But the independence spreading throughout Africa created different imperatives. Both Cameroons and Gabon became independent states and consequently put increased pressures on Spain to relinquish Spanish Guinea. Spanish authorities soon began to realize that it was time for a fresh look at Africa if they wanted to maintain and increase the influence of Hispanic culture and economy on this vast continent.

Thus, in late 1963, the policy of incorporating Guinea as a province of Spain was abandoned and a bill to introduce autonomy was approved by referendum. The nationalist leaders, including those advocating union with Cameroons, were invited to return to Guinea to take part in the referendum. As a policy decision, autonomous rule was a major step in the right direction.

Several factors lie at the root of Spain's increasing interest in the new Africa and her new posture. First, the North African Arab world has always been traditionally close to Spain. The Muslim invasions left a mark on Spanish life. The rich contributions of Arab art, architecture, music and even blood are interwoven throughout Hispanic culture. But it was not until 1950, when Franco's Spain announced the "bridge concept," that Spain developed a clear policy toward North

Africa. This concept holds that Spain could serve as a bridge between the Arab world and Western Europe—a special mission that would thereby enhance her position in both areas. Spain, with all her historical ties to North Africa, her present Saharan possessions, her cultural and geographical association and proximity, believes that she can be the mediator through which the Western world can communicate with North Africa and thereby halt Communist penetration of the Arab world.

Spain's policy has built on this tenet, which has met with both success and setback. It is in keeping with the Spanish desire for popularity and prestige and with the Spanish people's wish to export their culture. In addition, Spain, while European in outlook, is closer in living standard to the African and Asian nations than the more developed European countries. With its racial mixtures, Spain also provides a socially receptive atmosphere for Afro-Asian students.

Spain's new posture in regard to her colonies set the stage for greater cooperation between Spain and the rest of the African continent. With her new anti-colonial reputation, Spain can approach the Black African states with more prestige and hope of acceptance. There have already been exchanges of trade missions between Spain and the Congo, Cameroons, Gabon, Nigeria, Mauritania, Senegal and Tanzania, and several formal trade pacts have resulted.

Spain herself could be considered as having been an underdeveloped nation, for she has been the recipient of foreign aid, mainly from the United States. Recently, however, the AID mission was officially withdrawn from Spain in an atmosphere of success and accomplishment, terminating a long period of economic assistance. Although still plagued with many problems, Spain's economy can now look outward. Even while receiving aid herself, Spain was giving aid to others—mostly

her own colonies—on a very small scale. Now she is able to
pay more attention to these areas.

Religion and race probably are the two aspects of the
Spanish image most attractive to the Afro-Asian world.
English and American liberals, who criticize Spain's treatment
of Protestants, assume that their disdain is shared by Afro-
Asians. While not indifferent to this problem, Afro-Asians
place more emphasis on the tolerant treatment by the Spanish
of the followers of Islam. This has real meaning for them.
Muslim Arabs have always felt that Spain had a respect for
their way of life, and this feeling has been communicated by
the Arabs to other Afro-Asians. Since the overwhelming
majority of Afro-Asians are not Christians, they naturally
relate themselves more readily to Spain's treatment of non-
Christians than to her treatment of other Christians.

Furthermore, Afro-Asians, for the most part, "feel" that the
Spanish have at least less prejudice than Anglo-Saxon whites
toward non-whites. In Spain, as one African head of government told the author, there is far less feeling of racial superiority than in Anglo-Saxon countries. When asked for his
reasons, he said that he "just felt that way." This may not be
the scientific approach to problems but it is a reaction voiced
by many Afro-Asians. Thus, in the areas of religion and
race—two human problems charged with great emotion—
Spain has authentic credentials for carrying on a dialogue with
the new nations. Above all, in the eyes of the Afro-Asians,
Spain seems to be despised by her neighbors because of her
alleged backwardness and her population embracing peoples of
different colors. And, in fact, Edmund Burke, that old con-
servative, described Spain as "a huge whale stranded on the
shores of Europe."

The Spanish approach, in short, offers possibilities as a
model of a Western policy toward the Third World. In prin-

ciple, it fosters pride in things Spanish while respecting those values which the peoples of color themselves want to preserve. It is a policy shorn of racial superiority. By following in this path, Spain has an opportunity to benefit greatly—economically and politically as well as culturally—from the prestige to be gained by moving toward an important role in relations with the Third World.

Of all Western European nations, Ireland is in a most favorable position in regard to the Third World; indeed, Ireland has practically become an unofficial member of the Afro-Asian configuration at the United Nations. It is not a surprising place of preference, though little known in the United States.

Psychologically, the Irish have their own record of fighting fiercely for independence and they have viewed their battle in a broad perspective. More than eighty years ago, when few Westerners were promoting the cause of Afro-Asian nationalism, Ireland's historic figure, Charles Stewart Parnell, proclaimed that "the cause of nationality is sacred, in Asia and Africa as in Ireland."

The history of Ireland has marked the Irish people with a profound respect for independence unsurpassed by any other European country. For 700 years, Ireland chafed under the control of its colonial masters as most of the traditional Gaelic life was crushed and supplanted by that of the Norman invaders. Under British rule, English and Scottish landowners forced the Irish into serfdom. For 700 years, Irish defiance burst forth in boycotts, guerrilla warfare and rebellion, until the 1916 uprising proclaimed the Republic of Ireland. Finally, in 1937 a new constitution was adopted, making Ireland a sovereign, independent state. Ireland became a member of the League of Nations, and in 1955 was admitted into the United Nations. Its presence in the world body has been consistently

characterized by a strong independent policy and relentless
support of the right of self-determination.

The Irish position was presented with a flourish by Mr.
Frank Aiken, the Minister of External Affairs of Ireland, in a
speech before the United Nations in 1960:

I speak in this debate for the only Western European country
which has had experience, not just of temporary occupation, but
of a long historic epoch of foreign rule and of resistance to that
rule. We know what imperialism is and what resistance to it involves. We do not hear with indifference the voices of those
spokesmen of African and Asian countries who passionately
champion the right to independence of the millions who are still,
unfortunately, under foreign rule. On the contrary those voices
strike Irish hearts . . . tens of thousands of Irish people were sold
as slaves in the Barbadoes along with the peoples of Africa. . . .
We have laid aside bitterness regarding those dark days, but we
necessarily retain a historical memory of them, a memory which
gives us a sense of brotherhood with the newly-emerging peoples
of today.

Ireland has put its policy to work on behalf of the United
Nations and world peace. She has supplied to the UN peace-
keeping operations more soldiers in proportion to her popula-
tion than any other member state. Fifty Irish officers served
with the United Nations Observer Group in Lebanon, 12 Irish
officers served with the UN Truce Supervision Organization in
Palestine, and two Irish officers served with the UN Military
Observer team in west New Guinea. More than 4,000 Irish
soldiers served with the UN force in the Congo, where the
Chief of Staff of the Irish Army served as Commander in
Chief for more than a year. Ireland also had troops with the
UN force in Cyprus. Besides the military involvement, Irish-
men in increasing numbers are giving their talents to many of
the United Nations organizations.

The traditional manifestation of Irish involvement with
Africa and Asia has been missionary activity. It was Ireland's

first contact with the peoples of these areas. Irish priests, brothers and nuns not only proclaimed the Gospel, but also ministered to the human needs of the people, caring for the sick and educating the illiterate. The tradition has continued, for today there are over 4,000 Irish missionaries in Africa and almost 2,000 in Asia; that is, one out of every 750 Irish citizens is serving as a missionary in Africa or Asia.

In recent years, the missionary role has broadened to include many other services in keeping with Ireland's independent status. In the last few years, the Irish government has been asked by several African governments to help prepare civil servants on a short-term basis. In the field of education, Ireland has for a number of years attracted students to its universities from Africa and Asia, particularly from those areas where Irish missionaries were active. Despite rising numbers of Irish students, the National University of Ireland, Trinity College and the Royal College of Surgeons have continued to open their doors to students from the developing areas. Irish universities can now boast of outstanding Afro-Asian alumni in the service of their native countries.

More important than the skills available in Ireland is the attitude of the Irish people, which has attracted the Afro-Asian world to this small island republic for aid and assistance. Imbued with the spirit of nationalism and independence and familiar with the sufferings of a colonized people, the Irish readily identify themselves with the Africans and Asians. They can point to many events in their own history which seem to be repeating themselves in many of the new nations.

The Irish can recall exploitation by colonial landowners, and the death toll during the potato famine. They can describe how their fathers and uncles, and perhaps even themselves, formed guerrilla bands to harass their oppressors. They can tell of the prisons where their heroes died and where many of

their present leaders suffered. Many an African and Asian
leader has heard from the lips of an Irish priest the oratory of
Robert Emmet and Patrick Pearse in proclaiming the right of
the Irish people to the ownership of Ireland.

Afro-Asian leaders saw the tradition of Irish anti-imperi-
alism in operation at the United Nations. Ireland's "viewpoint
at the United Nations," her position on colonial problems and
participation in UN peace-keeping operations have given
added authenticity to her credentials as a "friend of the Third
World." While Ireland's role with the Afro-Asian states will be
limited by its resources as a small nation, her influence will
more and more surpass her means.

Among the Scandinavian countries of Sweden, Norway and
Denmark, contacts with the Third World have been mainly in
Africa. The underlying attraction for the African states is the
"middle way" of Scandinavia—socialism as a way of life.
African visitors to these countries have found that the implementation of socialism in the political, social and economic
fabric of the Scandinavian countries was attractive to them,
but the lack of "mysticism" has troubled some of them.

Sweden has been the most active in Africa among the
Scandinavian states. While her programs in Ethiopia and
Pakistan were not successful, the Swedish role in Tunisia has
been regarded as a success. The Tunisian leadership is
attracted to the pragmatic approach and the freedom from
ideology implicit in Swedish projects. In addition, Swedish
success in turning a poor country into a rich, mature economy
has impressed some Third World leaders. Tunisian President
Bourguiba in visiting Sweden in 1963 said, "When I travel in
Sweden, I think constantly: this country was poor also. A
hundred years ago and even much later, Sweden could not
feed her own sons and daughters. The speedy transformation
which has taken place among you permits us, too, to have
hope."

Student, intellectual and cultural groups, especially in Sweden and Denmark, have supported the independence aspirations of the African peoples. Moreover, African leaders have been well received on their visits to these countries, which are free of any colonial record. But the amount of technical assistance from Scandinavia to assist the African nations in their struggle against poverty, illiteracy and disease has been limited.

Germany, on the other hand, has launched a rather extensive aid program for the African states. The West German "Peace Corps" (actually called "Entwicklungsdienst"—developing service) had 451 volunteers serving in 16 countries in 1966—eight nations in Africa, four in Asia and four in Latin America. A goal of 2,000 volunteers working overseas by 1968 has been set. Aid projects have also been extended to Morocco, Tunisia, Libya, Tanzania and Cameroon.

German programs are welcomed as coming from a nation without a recent colonial past, though the dialogue between Germany and the Third World has been limited. The contacts seem mostly based on the fact that affluent Germany is prepared to aid the Afro-Asian states in their development programs. Another aspect of the German presence in the Afro-Asian world is the significantly increased amount of German assistance being given in Africa, Asia and Latin America through German Catholic and Protestant missionaries. While this aid is only beginning, it seems to have the human touch lacking in the official German government programs.

Although Churchill could haughtily announce that he had not become Prime Minister in order to preside over the dissolution of the British Empire, beginning with India, within ten years his successors had done just that. France, too, lost her possessions overseas. Now the future of Western European relations with the Third World will largely depend on the

manner in which the formerly dominant powers try to preserve their remaining interests in Africa and Asia. A significant and necessary step in creating a pattern of permanent
dialogue was taken when both of these major powers came to
terms with Afro-Asian nationalism.

Much, of course, will depend on developments in the remaining years of this decade. In the case of the French, the
key question is how deep and enduring is the unifying force of
French language and culture among former French depen-
dencies. The British position is endangered by her inability to
resolve the racial issues in her sphere of influence, southern
Africa, in favor of the African majority.

Fortunately, Afro-Asian response to Western Europe has
been to recognize that it is a mosaic of cultures, policies and
attitudes. This is manifested by the warm reaction of African
states to Spanish policies, the special affection that many Afro-
Asian leaders have for Ireland, and the special interest in the
Scandinavian countries.

In the present and future relationships between the various
European states and the Third World, there is a mixed com-
plement of factors and attitudes that prevent dialogue and also
lead to greater understanding and cooperation. The need for
greater understanding between the western European nations
and the Third World is clear. The question remains: Will
nations be dominated by events and memories or rise above
them in their pursuit of mutual understanding?

CHAPTER EIGHT

THE SPECIAL ROLES OF

THE VATICAN

AND ISRAEL

With the promulgation of Pope Paul VI's encyclical letter, "Populorum Progressio" on Easter Sunday, 1967, the concern of the Vatican for the Third World was set forth in unequivocal and dramatic terms. Its very first words were: "The development of peoples has the Church's close attention, particularly the development of those peoples who are striving to escape from hunger, misery, endemic diseases and ignorance; of those who are looking for a wider share in the benefits of civilization and a more active improvement of their human qualities; of those who are aiming purposefully at their complete fulfillment." Much of the significance of these sentiments lies in their origins. They emerge from a chain of similar concerns evident in "Rerum Novarum," issued by Pope Leo XIII in 1891, in "Quadregesimo Anno," issued by Pope Pius XII in

109

1931, and in Pope John's celebrated "Pacem in Terris" of 1963.

While this position of the Vatican emerges from a different background and set of circumstances than the position of Israel in the Third World, both are placed in special roles in the current formulas of world affairs. Neither powerful nor power-seeking in the mathematics of power politics, both made unique contributions in Asia and Africa. Born in 1948 out of a bitter war in a barren setting, Israel has become a model of national development much admired in the Third World. Israel as well as the Vatican has a worldwide constituency, adding another dimension to a discussion of their special roles.

While it is the Holy See and the Holy Father rather than the Catholic Church *per se* that have significant influence with the elite of the Afro-Asian world, the intrinsic relationship to the worldwide Catholic Church is clear. In their crusade against poverty, illiteracy and disease, Afro-Asian leaders find the Catholic Church allied with them. Thousands of Catholic priests, brothers and nuns are in the Afro-Asian countries as teachers, doctors, nurses and social service workers. And they are supported for the most part by financial aid obtained from Catholics in Western countries. Even Afro-Asian leaders who were critical of Church schools and hospitals in the pre-independence era have become the greatest admirers of what the Church is doing. There is also an awareness that the Church was not a "newcomer" to the struggle to improve life and learning in the Afro-Asian world. In fact, a majority of the Afro-Asian leaders, including those who are not Catholics, have attended Catholic schools at some time in their youth.

As one Muslim head of state told the author, Catholic missionaries "were here, are still with us and are not asking for more pay." He went on to point out that Catholic missionaries launched the first sanatorium for lepers in his country, and despite the international interest in the new nations, he is unable to find a non-missionary group to assume responsibility for the leper colony.

In the 1960s significant developments have enhanced the position of the Holy See with the Third World. Vatican Council II was the most dramatic, demonstrating to the Afro-Asian world the universal nature of the Church. On an almost daily basis Afro-Asians heard radio reports and read newspaper accounts of the assembly of 2,500 prelates discussing issues of importance to all. Through the drama of the Council, the international nature of the Catholic Church, her size and age, were etched in the minds of the Afro-Asian influentials observing the proceedings.

Moreover, Afro-Asians were participating in the Council. A non-Catholic head of state talked to me with pride of the leading role played by a bishop from his country in the discussions of several major issues. "Where else," the leader asked, "could a poor man from my country have a position of importance in an international organization deciding fundamental issues that would affect Europeans and Americans?"

During the time of the Council, the significance of the transfer of power to Afro-Asian bishops from European missionary bishops became obvious. Yellow, brown and black bishops demonstrated a partnership and a sharing of power with the white bishops from the larger Western countries. Official declarations of the Church have reflected the influence of the Afro-Asian bishops. All over the developing world, for example, there was a realization that a socialized society would not only be efficient economically, but could be built upon the traditional collectivity and common life of the people. The feelings of the Afro-Asian bishops and clergy were reflected in Pope John XXIII's encyclical "Mater et Magistra," which pointed out that it is natural for new nations to incorporate socialization into their socio-economic way of life.

Furthermore, the Catholic Church is the largest source of external non-governmental aid in many of the Afro-Asian countries. In countries struggling to meet operating budgets and seeking resources for educational and health projects, local Catholic bishops acquire an influence and prestige with the Afro-Asian rulers that they did not have when Europeans ran the local governments. In their driving determination to improve living conditions, Afro-Asians appreciate the active role of the Holy Father in assisting the peoples of color in their struggle for dignity.

The race factor also comes into the equation of the Holy See's relationship with the Afro-Asian world. An overpowering resentment against the continued practice of race superiority in various parts of the world causes the Afro-Asian world to respond strongly when the Holy See continues and expands its activities to end the scourge of racism. Whatever the abuses in practice, the mind of the Catholic Church has been clear on the race issue, and it can be traced in a revealing chain of official pronouncements from the early centuries. Undoubtedly, the rise to power of Afro-Asians in the Church as well as in the political sphere has given more urgency and emphasis to the racial teachings of Christianity. Pope John XXIII, aware of the changes taking place in the modern world, said in his historic encyclical "Pacem in Terris": "First among the rules of governing relations between political communities is that of truth. But truth requires elimination of every trace of racism, and the consequent recognition of the principle that all States are by nature equal in dignity."

The Vatican's concern for brotherhood was dramatized by Pope Paul VI's visits to India and the Holy Land. The impact was profound and reciprocal as set down in a moving Christmas address delivered by the Pope on December 22, 1965. Excerpts from that address convey the important intangibles in dealing with the Afro-Asian world—a sensitivity to their needs, their problems, their dignity and their individuality. The Pope's address is a remarkable example of such sensitivity. Speaking of the trip to Bombay, the Pope said:

We went forth as a foreigner and a pilgrim into a distant land unknown to us. We could have remained as an isolated foreigner, surrounded only by our brothers in the faith. Instead we met people, a festive, overflowing throng which seemed to us to represent not only the countless peoples of vast India, but also all the other Asian peoples. To be sure, they were not Catholic, but they were courteous, receptive, eager for a glance and a word from the strange visitor from Rome. It was indeed a moment of understanding and blending of many hearts.

What it is that these rejoicing crowds saw in us, we do not know. In them we saw a most worthy segment of humanity, one faithful to its millenary cultural traditions, not all Christian to be sure, but profoundly spiritual and in many respects humane and good, at once most ancient and youthful, today alive to and turned toward something which even the marvels of modern progress cannot provide, if they are not perhaps actually an obstacle.

Next the Pope drew the lesson of this experience, "a confirmation of what Christianity has been saying for centuries, and which the evolution of civilization has been slowly and gradually discovering and proclaiming: All men are brothers." Later in the address, the Pope drove home the point with a ringing indictment of racism, "which separates and opposes the different branches constituting the great human family, resulting in pride, mistrust, exclusivism, discrimination and sometimes even oppression, thus ruining the mutual respect and due esteem which ought to turn the diverse ethnical groups into a peaceful concert of brotherly peoples."

The visit of Pope Paul VI to the United Nations following his visits to Bombay and the Holy Land had profound impact

on the Afro-Asian world. When His Holiness arrived at the
United Nations on October 4, 1965, he was on display before
the leadership of the world gathered there and before millions
over radio and television. The Afro-Asian world responded
warmly and with enthusiasm to what they saw and heard: a
worldwide force free from cold-war involvements rallying the
world to peace and international social justice. The Afro-
Asians experienced a shared determination to avoid war and
to end the horrible gap in living standards between the developed and developing societies.

Pope Paul's visit to the United Nations strengthened his
position as an independent moral force representing universal
social justice. Afro-Asian leaders now regard the Holy See as
an institution quite distinct from the Western powers. The
leaders of the new nations find themselves in a difficult, cold
world and are comforted by the emergence of the Holy Father
as a strong and independent moral force. Pope Paul reaffirmed
his non-aligned role at an opportune moment after his United
Nations visit. At a time when the Pope's efforts to resolve the
war in Vietnam were becoming a significant factor in international politics and gaining a strong response among Afro-
Asians, the Holy See's reception for diplomats was held in
early January 1966. The Pope used the occasion to make it
clear that his peace efforts were totally independent of "the
competitions of this world."

By well-timed, sensitive statements and by discreet diplomatic deeds, Pope Paul is carrying on the active role of the
Holy See in pursuing rapport with the Third World and in
furthering world peace. In mid-1966, the Pope's message to
the second session of the Governing Council of the United
Nations Development Program set forth the three prongs of
Vatican policy. They have a particular resonance in the
nations of the Third World, for the Pope cites "a threefold

hunger to be satisfied"—arising from "physical, intellectual and spiritual poverty."

The Pope places the problem in the broadest possible context by declaring that the "whole world must become aware that poverty is not only an intolerable evil for its victim, but must also be so considered by every man worthy of the name." The import of his statement must be gauged by the fact that it is addressed particularly to developed nations, which must understand the situation in the Third World, and it comes from a voice which commands attention. It is difficult to surpass the following statement by Pope Paul calling attention to worldwide poverty:

Man must indeed be enabled to survive, but he must also be given the means of living fully, as a person capable of founding a family and giving his children a satisfactory upbringing; these are the tasks that call for the disinterested help of all men of goodwill, surpassing all differences of nation, race, culture and religion. Moreover, the man of today ought to become more convinced of this as each day passes; it is his own existence that is at stake, and not optional assistance and emergency aid. All human resources must be mobilized, and it is not enough to give of one's possessions; one must give of the best of oneself. The peace to which the world aspires will be built only at this price because, as has rightly been said, "development is the new name for peace."

In its way, Israel reflects the Pope's concern. As a small nation which survives by combining determination and skill, Israel offers sensitivity to the plight of the Afro-Asian world. A people of historic adversity, the Israelis begin with a psychological response to the needs of the Afro-Asians and reach practical benefits for both the giver and the receiver.

In fact, sensitivity to Afro-Asian needs was expressed by the founder of Zionism, Theodor Herzl. He wrote of the Jewish state he envisaged: "In our country we shall set up a great University to which students will come from Africa and Asia."

He went on to declare that only a people that have suffered as the Jews have in their centuries of diaspora could understand the need to make independence a reality for the people of Africa and Asia.

As reflected in Herzl's statement on Asia and Africa, Israel has a passionate and almost inborn humanitarian drive to help those who have been denied and persecuted. Its dedication to the principles of racial equality lies at the root of a readiness to communicate knowledge and experience that will help others to break the bonds of impoverishment.

The approach to the Third World of the Afro-Asian peoples is rooted in the Israeli psyche and experience. Israel itself was an impoverished country when it became independent, but as Herzl said, "If you will it, it is no dream." The Israelis have an overpowering confidence in the ability of man to help himself and they have experienced the dignity and joy of working toward self-sufficiency. No matter how much financial and technical assistance is poured into the land, only the people can transform it.

Israel is an attractive model for the new nations. Upon visiting Israel, they have been especially impressed by the pioneer spirit and dynamism of the people as well as the dramatic achievements within less than two decades of independence.

Israel faced similar problems of nation-building. It had to create unity and coherence out of a varied and expanding population. Hundreds of thousands of Jewish refugees have entered Israel, nearly tripling the population since independence. Less than one-third of the present population is native-born; the remaining two-thirds come from more than 100 countries.

This populace, embodying vastly different languages and cultures and including Arab and Christian minorities, presented a monumental problem of unification. Moreover, it had a high proportion of professionals and a deficiency of agricultural and industrial skills. The problems parallel those of the new nations, with their proliferation of tribes and shortage of necessary skills.

In absorbing newcomers, the Israeli government successfully drew many to the settlement areas and rural villages, so that the numbers were sufficiently dispersed, leaving only one-third of the population in the major cities. This achievement alone has tremendous significance for the Afro-Asian states, in which rising expectations have drawn rural people into the already overcrowded cities.

Israel has also solved the problem of foreign aid. It has received technical assistance from the major powers, as have most of the Afro-Asian states. It has worked out suitable plans to utilize this assistance to the fullest by adjusting advanced scientific knowledge and aid to local needs and conditions. While conditions may be different in the new nations, the Israeli government has developed the know-how for mobilizing national resources in national programs.

In transforming their underdeveloped country, the Israelis resorted to various forms of enterprise without jeopardizing individual liberty. Their flexible approach has allowed the development of the socialistic collective farms of the kibbutz, public utilities and national companies, along with private enterprise. This variety is highly attractive to the Third World leader, who is sometimes pressured into a simplistic choice between the capitalistic interests of the West and the socialistic ideology of the East.

One characteristic of the Israeli assistance program which is cited often in the new nations is that it carries no obvious political strings. Although Israel avoids participation in the cold-war conflict, it does sometimes pose a problem to the Afro-

Asian states who need or want to maintain close relationships with the Arab states.

At first, great pressure was exerted by the Arab states to isolate Israel. However, most Afro-Asian states have asserted their independence and followed their policy of non-alignment, even in the Arab-Israeli struggle. In general, most leaders of the new nations believe in the necessity to negotiate the differences between the Arabs and Israelis, and they could have a decisive influence in eventually bringing the two factions to the conference table.

Being a small and relatively poor nation, Israel cannot afford large-scale assistance programs, grants and loans. Thus its international cooperation program is built along the lines of its own resources—the provision of technical experts and scholarships. Since its programs are small, it is able to provide personalized and tailor-made projects.

Between 1958 and 1963 Israel took part in cooperative projects in almost 100 countries, sending more than 1,000 experts overseas. These included medical doctors, agricultural specialists, educators, engineers and economists. One of the most important features is that these projects are self-liquidating. Afro-Asian replacements are trained to take over completely.

A unique and successful form of venture has been the joint company. Israel has joined with several Afro-Asian governments in forming various companies. Local personnel are trained on the job to fill the technical and managerial positions needed to operate the enterprise. Then the participating government buys out the Israeli investment and takes full control when it is ready and able. One such company is Ghana's Black Star Shipping Lines, which is run in conjunction with Israel's Zim Lines. The Ghanaian government has since bought out the Israeli shares, but retained Israeli management.

Another aspect of the assistance program is technical train-ing and education scholarships. The annual turnover of stu-dents coming to Israel is about 2,500. There are approxi-mately 90 courses a year, covering agriculture, education, vocational training, nursing, labor unions, administration and community development. The students learn mostly by doing, with practical training in fields, laboratories, hospitals and factories. Although the emphasis is on short-term intensive courses lasting a few months to a year, there are also six-year medical programs and regular academic programs in the col-leges and universities.

In addition, there are tailor-made programs to provide training in specialized fields for individuals with specific needs. In this program, the student often studies under the tutorship of a professional craftsman or agency. Thus the Israeli government is ready to provide any type of training which is necessary and useful to the country concerned.

Although almost every phase of Israeli life and government is utilized in this aid program, a few relate particularly to the Afro-Asian situation and specific needs. For example, the Israeli labor movement set up an Afro-Asian Institute for Labor Studies and Cooperation, which is designed to include trained unionists and co-op workers as well as government officials dealing with labor and cooperative unions. Since the labor movement in Israel played an important part in develop-ing the country and since the emphasis is on the rural aspects of unionism, the Israeli experience has much to offer the new nations developing their own cooperative and worker units.

The Israeli Ministry of Defense has provided a special training ground and example in the Fighting Pioneer Youth, a unique unit in the army. The African states especially find the unit applicable to their own needs, for it combines military security with youthful enthusiasm. Half the time is spent in military instruction and half in communal and development activities.

Out of such contacts and pinpointed assistance, the Israelis have developed an influential position in the Afro-Asian countries. This is supported by extensive diplomatic involvement with resident ambassadors in most African and Asian states— a considerable feat for a small nation. Though Israeli ambassadors often have staffs of only two or three, their embassies are generally regarded by both diplomats and journalists as among the best informed sources in Afro-Asian capitals. For the Israelis, success in achieving relations with the Afro-Asian countries represents a back door out of the ring of belligerence created by Arab hostility. For the Afro-Asians, the Israelis represent skilled, sensitive sources of assistance.

Taken together, Israel and the Vatican represent a significant and promising development in world affairs. In what might be called a diplomatic division of labor, each is making a constructive contribution that stems from its particular focus and its specific capacities. More important, both have been able to make a contribution that benefits the goals both of those who give and of those who receive. The result is power in a positive and promising sense—the strength to help oneself by helping others.

In their own and different ways the Holy See and Israel have special roles in world affairs and in regard to the Third World. While important to the Third World for the power and influence they have, the Holy See and Israel are also as separate from the Third World as they are from major power blocs.

CHAPTER NINE

THE UNITED NATIONS:

MIRROR OF THE

THIRD WORLD

Every September each new General Assembly of the United Nations unfolds another chapter in the postwar rise of the Third World and the revolutionary changes in international affairs. Today, any observer standing at the top of the escalator used by United Nations delegates at the General Assembly building in New York can read—in microcosm —the story of Afro-Asian emergence in the sight of a turban, a sari, or a boubou. It is like holding up a mirror to the emergence of the Third World.

By 1955, the tenth anniversary of the United Nations, the late Dag Hammarskjöld cited in his annual report "the great upheaval in the relationship of nations and peoples that is under way" and pointed out that "the peoples of Asia today, and of Africa tomorrow, are moving toward a new relation-

121

ship with what history calls the West." By 1957, as the pace of change quickened, Mr. Hammarskjöld reported: "The United Nations reflects, but is in no sense a cause of, the renaissance of Asia. The awakening of Africa, and the other great changes that are under way in the balance of power and relationships of the peoples are likewise part of the dynamic of history itself. As always, they bring with them many grave problems of adjustment."

The mirror threw back a much different image from that of 1945, when the UN was mainly a white man's club. The United Nations came into existence at that time mainly as an instrument for the West, led by the United States, and the East, led by the Soviet Union, to resolve their disputes without resorting to war. The peoples of color who in 1945 constituted the majority of the world's population were hardly represented. By the time the United Nations celebrated its twentieth anniversary in 1965, this situation had significantly changed —from 11 Afro-Asian states present in 1945 to 65 members in 1967. And the four new nations of the Caribbean that are inhabited predominantly by the peoples of color also can be added to the Third World.

The change in the power equation from a white West-Soviet formula to a more universal institution was symbolized in 1964 when the nineteenth General Assembly was under an Asian-African triumvirate: a Black African, Alex Quaison-Sackey, as President, and two Asians, Secretary-General U Thant and Under Secretary C. V. Narasimhan.

The presence of the Third World in the United Nations has turned it into a truly universal institution. The point was made dramatically by Pope Paul VI on his visit to the United Nations on October 4, 1965, when he declared: "Permit us to congratulate you on having had the wisdom to open this Assembly to the young peoples, to the States which have recently attained independence and national freedom. Their presence here is the proof of the universality and magnanimity which inspire the principles of this institution."

The Afro-Asian countries listed on p. 124 are now members of the United Nations.

These nations, however great their differences as individual countries, are drawn together by three compelling centripetal forces:

1. Issues for war, peace and disarmament. The Third World insists on remaining neutral and non-aligned and forcefully supports all efforts to achieve disarmament.

2. Efforts to eliminate racism and colonialism. The Third World regards all aspects of racism and colonialism as anathema and, regardless of other considerations, supports projects and policies opposed to these doctrines.

3. Development. The Afro-Asian states are joined by many of the Latin American members in an obsession to end the triple curse of poverty, illiteracy and disease.

Once the impact of the new nations was felt at the United Nations, a significant change in the items under discussion on the annual General Assembly Agenda could be observed. The Third World brought into the halls of the United Nations the poor man and made him a topic of concern for the major powers.

Meanwhile, the Third World countries have articulated at the United Nations their view of neutrality, which they insist is a positive rather than a negative approach to world problems. In the major conflicts between East and West, the Afro-Asian nations invariably strive to avoid taking sides. Sometimes they will apply the leverage of their large voting powers to seek accommodations, for they represent approximately half the total membership and, if united, can effectively control any

AFRICAN	ASIAN
1. Algeria	1. Afghanistan
2. Burundi	2. Burma
3. Cameroon	3. Cambodia
4. Central African Republic	4. Ceylon
5. Chad	5. China*
6. Congo—Brazzaville	6. India
7. Congo (Dem. Rep. of)	7. Indonesia
8. Dahomey	8. Iran*
9. Ethiopia*	9. Iraq*
10. Gabon	10. Israel
11. Ghana	11. Japan
12. Guinea	12. Jordan
13. Ivory Coast	13. Kuwait
14. Kenya	14. Laos
15. Liberia*	15. Lebanon*
16. Libya	16. Malaysia
17. Madagascar	17. Maldive Islands
18. Malawi	18. Mongolia
19. Mali	19. Nepal
20. Mauritania	20. Pakistan
21. Morocco	21. Philippines*
22. Niger	22. Saudi Arabia*
23. Nigeria	23. Singapore
24. Rwanda	24. Syrian Arab Republic*
25. Senegal	25. Thailand
26. Sierra Leone	26. Turkey*
27. Somalia	27. Yemen
28. Sudan	

CARIBBEAN

AFRICAN	CARIBBEAN
29. Togo	1. Haiti*
30. Tunisia	2. Jamaica
31. Uganda	3. Trinidad and Tobago
32. United Arab Republic*	4. Guyana
33. United Republic of Tanzania	5. Barbados
34. Upper Volta	
35. Zambia	
36. Gambia	
37. Botswana	
38. Lesotho	

* Denotes Charter Member of the U.N.

outcome in the General Assembly. In the 1960s, this became increasingly significant as the center of power at the United Nations tended to shift from the Security Council, where the major powers dominate, to the General Assembly, where the Third World countries represent the major power.

A characteristic description of Third World policy was enunciated by Prince Norodom Sihanouk of Cambodia when he discussed the difference between neutrality and neutralism and the misunderstanding of what they involved. Writing in *Foreign Affairs* in July 1958, he maintained: "In our foreign relations we have favored neutrality, which in the United States is all too often confused with 'neutralism', although it is fundamentally different. We are neutral in the same way Switzerland and Sweden are neutral—not neutralist like Egypt or Indonesia."

Besides the confrontation between East and West which has troubled the United Nations, there is the confrontation between Western powers and their former colonies. With the exceptions already noted in southern Africa, the confrontation has usually been harmonious at the United Nations. On this count, the United States has played a major part, dramatically summarized by the late President Kennedy when he addressed the United Nations on September 25, 1961. He cited the progress made since the end of World War II: one billion people and 9 million square miles transformed into 42 free and independent states. Then he added:

I do not ignore the remaining problems of traditional colonialism which still confront this body. Those problems will be solved, with patience, good will and determination. Within the limits of our responsibility in such matters, my Country intends to be a participant and not merely an observer, in the peaceful expeditious movement of nations from the status of colonies to the partnership of equals. That continuing tide of self-determination which runs so strong, has our sympathy and our support.

While the Afro-Asian bloc has functioned more like a group than a solid bloc at the United Nations, the colonial issue produces solidarity. It is so closely wedded to the immediate experience of Third World nations and so prominent a factor in their domestic public opinion that it predominates in their foreign policy. G. L. Mehta, formerly Indian Ambassador to the United States, has said: "In Asia and Africa, the principal criterion for judging international policies is whether they help towards the liberation of peoples and towards the stability of their countries."

Beyond this issue, there are varieties of responses among Third World nations, and there are what might be called degrees of neutrality. In Asia, India and Japan represent two distinct types, with the latter leaning more closely to the West along with the Philippines and Thailand. On the other hand, Indian neutrality is more attractive to countries like Cambodia and Indonesia which periodically express views critical of the West. In Africa, Mali and Tunisia represent a range of neutral reactions, with Mali leaning to the Communist bloc and Tunisia openly sympathetic to the West.

The grouping of Third World countries into the so-called Afro-Asian bloc is further complicated by a network of alliances, associations and commitments at the United Nations. They can be silhouetted as shown in Table 2.

The results of Table 2's network of diplomatic involvements can be illustrated by examining the seven roll-call votes in the Fifteenth General Assembly—one on Chinese representation, four on Congo problems and two on Cuba. The so-called neutralists and other non-aligned and uncommitted nations were conspicuous for their lack of "bloc voting." India, for example, was followed by only one member state, Ceylon, and on all but one roll call, by only two others (Burma and Indonesia). The United Arab Republic, chief aspirant to Arab

TABLE 2. ASSOCIATIONS OF AFRO-ASIAN MEMBERS OF THE U.N. THAT SOMETIMES INFLUENCE VOTES[a]

Soviet Bloc		Western Bloc

ASIAN MEMBERS

Mongolia		Turkey

Soviet Bloc	French Language	Commonwealth
Afghanistan Burma China Iran Israel Japan Philippines Thailand	Cambodia Laos	Ceylon India Malaysia Maldive Islands Pakistan Singapore

Arab Group

Iraq	Lebanon
Jordan	Syria
Kuwait	Yemen
Saudi Arabia	

AFRICAN MEMBERS

Soviet Bloc		French Language	Commonwealth
Ethiopia Liberia Somalia	Algeria Libya Tunisia Morocco Sudan United Arab Republic	Burundi Cameroon Central African Rep. Chad Congo (Brazza.) Congo (Dem. Rep.) Dahomey Gabon Guinea Ivory Coast Madagascar Mali Mauritania Niger Rwanda Senegal Togo Upper Volta	Ghana Kenya Malawi Nigeria Sierra Leone Uganda Zambia Botswana Lesotho Gambia

[a] *Note*: This chart is intended only to indicate some of the larger groupings; it does not include such bilateral relationships as the historic friendship between the United States and Liberia.

127

leadership, was supported consistently by only three states (Iraq, Yemen and Afghanistan), and by only one other (Saudi Arabia) on all but one of the test votes. Nigeria was supported by only one African state, Ethiopia, on all roll calls.

A United Nations study, in commenting on this Afro-Asian voting pattern, said, "The most striking trait among the Independents was the disposition to avoid taking sides in the contest between the rival power blocs. There were eight Independents which recorded their abstention or did not vote at all in the contest between the two rival power blocs. There were eight Independents which recorded their abstention or did not vote at all in a majority or more of the seven test votes. They were Finland, Cambodia, Laos, Liberia, the Central African Republic, Cameroon, Congo (Brazzaville) and the Dominican Republic. There were a dozen member states which abstained in as many as three of these test votes. Few of these states regarded the rivalry between Washington and Moscow as matters of primary concern to themselves. Many of them regarded as more important the clash of interests between themselves and the Colonial powers."[1]

For the United States, the voting patterns of the Third World countries represent a clear test of whether its foreign policy is remaining in touch with the majority non-white, underdeveloped peoples of the world. In one place and at one time, United States foreign policy is tested at each United Nations debate and at each United Nations roll call. Also, in that worldwide forum, American attitudes and aims can be presented and explained with results that can be persuasive.

But there is also a danger and, fortunately, it is visible. If the United States were regularly in the minority at the United

---

[1] Commission to Study the Organization of Peace, *The UN Secretary General, His Role in World Politics*, pp. 10, 11.

Nations, there would be clear evidence of a decline in its world position. Foreign policy cannot always win a popularity contest. But if the United States is going to compete successfully in an ideological contest with the Communist world and if it is going to espouse its democratic ideals effectively, then an agonizing reappraisal would be needed if the UN, particularly the Third World countries, consistently rejected United States positions.

It is a danger pointed up by Thomas Hovet, Jr., who has written an authoritative analysis of bloc voting at the United Nations:

> One is forced to consider with some misgivings the future role of the United States in the United Nations. Virtually all the members of the many delegations who express their concern mention what they call the "failures" of the United States with reluctance. And yet the sense of distrust, or at least doubt, appears to be increasing as the various delegations develop increasing degrees of rapport and intimate contacts with other delegations, the members of which recognize the alteration of diplomatic negotiation techniques which are demanded in the bloc and group structure of the United Nations.[2]

In the context of the various groupings at the UN, flexibility and foresight are needed more than ever by the major powers, for the non-white majority now has a decisive role in what was once the white man's club. To maintain its success pattern in the first twenty years of the UN, the United States must constantly keep the new power equation in mind.

For the Third World nations, the United Nations is a unique opportunity and a special instrument. Through their permanent missions to the UN they are able to maintain contact with fellow Third World countries without the heavy commitment of men and money to diplomatic missions in all

[2] Thomas Hovet, Jr., *Bloc Politics in the United Nations* (Cambridge, Massachusetts: Harvard University Press, 1960), p. 119.

these countries. Thus most Afro-Asian states assign their leading diplomats to the UN post.

More important, the United Nations is the only place in the world where the influence of these countries outweighs their economic and military strength. And it is through the Secretariat and the Secretary-General that their influence is particularly felt. This strength was clearly evident in the arrangements for the visit of Pope Paul VI to the UN in October 1965. The Third World nations enthusiastically supported the visit because they felt that the Pope would add the prestige and influence of the Holy See in support of their three central concerns: war, peace and disarmament; efforts to eliminate racism and colonialism; aid programs to reduce poverty, illiteracy and disease. As expected, Pope Paul's visit was significant on all three counts.

The support being given to the Third World nations at the UN by the Holy See and other international religious and humanitarian groups has influenced the whole complex of the United Nations—from the offices of the Secretary-General and specialized agencies to the periphery of non-governmental bodies. All three central concerns of the Third World are now in the forefront of UN interest. This is a far cry from the grim predictions that the admission of these "small, poor states" would distract the UN from the major problems facing the world in favor of the narrow interests of these few countries. The opposite has happened: the Third World has humanized the United Nations and sustained a larger view of a world struggling to achieve the vision of mankind ever evolving toward a better life for all.

CHAPTER TEN

THE WEST, THE 1970s AND

THE THIRD WORLD

Western policy during the 1970s will involve a confrontation more challenging than a single ideology and more potent than a single power bloc. It is the confrontation with constant and continuing change—change at home and abroad, changes in the technological, social, economic, political and religious areas of living. Meeting this challenge of change will nowhere be more formidable than in the countries of the Third World.

This is the appropriate starting point for any projection of Western policy with the Third World. Change is more than the beginning fact of global life; it is the context within which the West must pursue its goals in international affairs. Any foreign policy that is not geared to the phenomenon of change will be constantly suffering real (or imaginary) setbacks and will squander resources which the West can provide and the Third World needs desperately.

The lesson of change has become a commonplace theme in

131

relations with the Communist bloc—with worldwide reper-
cussions. Stalin's implacable Russia gave way to Khrushchev's
impulsive and erratic Russia. Most revealing of all, the solid
Communist bloc of nations has been consistently eroded; this
process was climaxed by the thundering differences between
Red China and the rest of the Communist world. Not that
Communism has stopped being a threat, but it has become a
threat expressing itself in different and variable dimensions.
Changes have taken place, changes that only a few years ago
would have been inconceivable. This, of course, drastically
affects the East-West conflict as reflected in the Third World.

Beneath the surface of diplomatic strategy and tactics, the
abiding reality is the transformation taking place in all Third
World countries. The pace varies—from the dramatic
modernization of Japan and the prosperity of the Ivory Coast
to the backwardness of Afghanistan and the poverty of Upper
Volta. Each Third World country is experiencing the worldwide explosion of knowledge and technology, but for each it is
a much more traumatic experience than in the West. The
emerging countries have much farther to go in modernization
than the West and are lacking in human, financial, technical
and social resources. And they are newly independent, still
harboring the hang-over of colonialism while still lacking the
apparatus of modernized states.

Yet these countries are crowding so much into the concentrated postwar period of independence and throwing all their
energies into a gigantic commitment to national progress.
They are striving for political, social, economic and technological stability—all at the same time.

Primarily, the Third World countries demand that the West
join in the commitment to eradicate poverty, illiteracy and
disease. This commitment must be in the forefront of any
effective Western foreign policy with the Third World. All

assets of the West must be mobilized in what is clearly the most crucial task facing the West in the second half of the twentieth century: working with the Third World to eliminate the terrible gap in living standards between the "have" and "have-not" countries. After generating an esprit among its own people, the United States must work closely and harmoniously with the major and smaller European states so that the treasurehouse of Western assets are energized in this noble effort.

To expect this movement to develop worldwide momentum without the sustained leadership of the President of the United States would not be realistic. Here is an example of the noble use of power. The American President, from his pinnacle of power, must call forth all assets of the Western community and inspire the Third World in a global enterprise of unprecedented scope.

The Afro-Asian leadership must also assume responsibility for *directing* and *doing,* for this must be a partnership in which all participate and work together. The desire to avoid paternalism must be present in the Third World as well as in the Western nations. The Afro-Asian leaders must develop a driving determination to analyze their own situations realistically and develop plans and methods designed to bring the fundamental ingredients of the good life to their peoples. While the obsession for rapid change has been present in the Afro-Asian world, basic research and planning have often been lacking. Without sound blueprints, the goals of progress will not be translated into viable projects and substantial results.

While Third World leaders have a responsibility to use aid realistically and efficiently, the major responsibility for ways and means of providing aid must be faced by the West as the source of such aid. The West, and particularly the United

States, must adopt enlightened criteria in answering the sensitive and complex question of who gets what kind of aid and how much. While the following considerations do not constitute an exhaustive list, they suggest the ingredients of an effective approach in the immediate future.

1. Aid should not be utilized to purchase "friends" and allies. This has an obvious drawback: it does not work. Such "aid with strings," as it has been denigrated in the Afro-Asian world, has almost always failed to guarantee the friendship of any country and certainly is subject to the dangers of changing regimes, a common phenomenon in the new countries.

2. Aid should be tailor-made to the receiving country. One government's salvation may be another's downfall. Whereas one country may need hydroelectric dams to accelerate industrialization, another may need roads and harbor facilities. Here, close collaboration between Western experts and experts in the receiving countries is crucial.

3. Aid should be withheld where it encourages and serves delusions of grandeur on the part of a country's leadership—without benefiting national development.

4. Both short-term and long-term planning should be applied, depending on the circumstances and conditions in the receiving country.

5. Aid should be fully integrated into the development of the country and should in no way unbalance national planning or distort any sound program of priorities.

6. There should be reasonable assurance that the aid will be used for the purposes given and that no major abuses will undermine its effective application. At the same time, it is necessary to take local conditions and standards of efficiency into consideration. But it is not sensible to tolerate high-level corruption in connection with Western aid.

A notable application of this approach is evident in the Food for Peace program or the Food for Freedom program, as President Johnson preferred to call it. A significant innovation in the 1966 version of the program was the requirement that nations receiving food give evidence of plans or intentions to expand their own food production. By injecting this self-help condition, the United States was not only endorsing a partnership concept. It was making it a pre-condition of technical and economic aid as well, for the race against worldwide famine must be run by all countries.

In the case of the United States, the trend of its aid policies has been consistent since a shift in attitude crystallized under President Kennedy. As noted earlier, the John Foster Dulles policy of dividing countries into those for or against us has given way to primary concern about the welfare and progress of Third World countries as the best source of Western security and the most effective bulwark against Communism.

By the end of the 1960s, a further refinement—which this author has frequently heard discussed in official circles—was clarified and pinpointed. A significant public expression was a report submitted to President Johnson by Edward M. Korry, United States Ambassador to Ethiopia. While the report singled out Africa, its main tenets—approved by President Johnson—are applicable to all Third World countries. The three main tenets are selective allotment of aid, encouragement of regionalism, and confidence that the emerging countries realize Communism is no panacea. Each tenet can be viewed in terms of the material developed in the previous chapters. In my view, they should be applied to the Third World countries along the following lines:

Selective Aid. Aid should be allotted where it can have maximum effect in combating the triple curse of poverty, illiteracy and disease. This means that each country's need and ability to use aid must be calculated and aid must be available according to the situation in the receiving country. It should be given to countries in need of broad-scale support and also in times of economic or agricultural crisis. At the same time, attention must be paid to those pivotal countries which occupy key roles because of their position, power or leadership. The countries that suffer from acute and chronic shortages of water are good examples of how concentration on discovering sources of water sufficient to meet the minimum needs of the countries would be more sensible than scattering the aid among a variety of projects.

Encourage Regionalism. Instead of ignoring fragmentation, the West should attempt to reward cooperation across national borders by making aid available for joint national projects. Out of such beginnings in practical cooperation more far-reaching results will be achieved. Developing sources of electrical power from the major rivers that transverse several countries is a good example of regional assistance.

Western Confidence. As discussed earlier, the wave of Communism that beats against the shores, the borders and cities of Asia and Africa is by no means irresistible. In fact, the lack of Communist success in Africa and its setbacks in Asia underline the independence of Third World countries in the worldwide power equation. In 1966 there were reminders everywhere of how ephemeral the Communist inroads were. Not only did Indonesia turn its back on the Chinese Communists; even North Korea opted for "independent communism" —in an expression of Titoism Asian-style. In various African states Chinese Communist emissaries were ousted, and in Ghana Kwame Nkrumah was deposed while pursuing his Chinese courtship in Peking.

But none of this takes place in a vacuum. The United States, as leader of the West, must recognize the importance that the Third World attributes to the avoidance of war between the major powers. The Afro-Asians regard it as sacrilegious that both the major Western powers and the Sino-Soviets are spending a major part of their national incomes on war materials. They not only expect the major power blocs to avoid nuclear confrontation, but also to reduce systematically the amounts of money being spent on armaments. While the United States cannot be expected to abdicate its responsibilities as guardian of the West against Sino-Soviet attack, this country still is expected by the Afro-Asian world to carry on—undiminished—its disarmament and peace campaign.

Furthermore, the United States must take greater cognizance of the predominant Afro-Asian opinion on Vietnam. The American military presence in Vietnam by the end of the mid-1960s had seriously impaired the United States image with the Afro-Asian peoples. All the explanations of fighting aggression and keeping faith with treaties have had little or no impact on the Third World. This is not to say that there is no validity to official Washington explanations for the post-1963 military build-up. But one aspect of the United States role in Vietnam is clear: the longer the United States continues its military presence in this Southeast Asian country the greater will be the deterioration of Afro-Asian respect for the integrity of the American position in world affairs.

At home, the United States must assert its world leadership role by demonstrating racial harmony and cultural pluralism. It is the necessary American demonstration of the sincerity of its foreign policy. It is the fact behind the image. The American President must continue to reaffirm the nation's wholehearted commitment to the reality of equality and mobilize all forces to bring that reality closer. America must do this because it is the right thing to do, but it is also true that without such an effort and without dramatic results, the American voice will be enfeebled in the Third World countries.

A comprehensive blueprint for future relationships between the West and the Third World was given to the world by Pope Paul VI in his encyclical "Populorum Progressio" on Easter Sunday, 1967. In forthright language, he pointed out that the phenomenon of the rich growing richer while the poor remain poor carries with it the threat of violence. Rich nations, he said, must bear the cost of developing the nations of the Third World—"otherwise the continued greed of the rich nations could only provoke the judgment of God and the wrath of the poor with consequences no one can foretell."

The full significance of the papal document was in its overall appeal that mankind remove the causes of alienation and strive for greater harmony. The future policy of the West toward the Third World should be rooted in one of the closing paragraphs of the historic encyclical:

All of us who have heard the appeal of suffering peoples, all of you who are working to answer their cries, you are the apostles of a development which is good and genuine, which is not wealth that is self-centered and sought for its own sake, but rather an economy which is put at the service of man, the bread which is daily distributed to all, as a sign of brotherhood and a sign of Providence.

. . . For, if the new name for peace is development, who would not wish to labor for it with all his powers.

More than ever before, foreign policy in the 1970s will be oriented to the future, particularly in the Third World countries which are rushing to create a new and dramatically better tomorrow for their people. Indeed, it is that orientation to the future which characterizes the only foreign policy worthy of the United States. And it is the drive toward development that will predominate in that future.

In this regard, the voice of Teilhard de Chardin has the universal ring and the philosophical resonance that ultimately can be expressed in foreign policy. For foreign policy to succeed in the modern "global village" in which mankind lives, it must be humanistic in means and ends, methods and goals. Chardin, the Jesuit philosopher, has underlined three aspirations as "characteristic of a faith in the future":

> a passion for the future,
> a passion for the universal
> and a passion for the individual

Such aspirations define a worthy foreign policy, a human policy for the West, led by the United States, in regard to the Third World in the coming decade.

APPENDICES

Appendix I is from a message sent by Pope Paul VI to the Governing Council of the United Nations Development Program on June 6, 1966, in Milan, Italy, and also includes the reply from Secretary-General U Thant. This exchange of messages is one of the numerous examples of growing dialogue between the Holy See and the Third World and the Holy See and the United Nations.

Appendix II consists of an address to the United Nations delivered by the President of the Republic of Zambia, Dr. Kenneth David Kaunda, on November 15, 1966.

In Appendices III and IV two African diplomats express themselves on the subject of the relationships between the West and the Third World. Appendix III was originally the main part of an address given by Ousmane Soce Diop, Ambassador and Permanent Representative of the Republic of Senegal to the United Nations, speaking at the University of Carbondale, Illinois, on October 21, 1965. Appendix IV represents the core of an address given by Chief S. O. Adebo, Ambassador and Permanent Representative of Nigeria to

140

the United Nations, at Fordham University on March 1, 1966, where he also had the degree of Ll.D. (honoris causa) conferred upon him.

Appendix V is devoted to the positive and negative factors affecting dialogue between the West and the Peoples of Color. This was originally the principal part of an address delivered by Thomas Patrick Melady at Manhattan College on June 14, 1966.

APPENDIX I

Message of Pope Paul VI
to the Governing Council of the
United Nations Development Program

June 6, 1966

The United Nations Development Program, carrying on the work formerly financed and administered by the Expanded Program of Technical Assistance and the United Nations Special Fund, is bending its efforts to expedite the economic and social development of backward countries. How can We not but rejoice to see competent and responsible men joining together to pool the resources given to them by the international community of nations for the purpose of promoting the physical, intellectual and spiritual progress of the less favoured of its members?

It is, in fact, man as one complete entity whom development seeks to improve harmoniously, and there is therefore a threefold hunger to be satisfied at a time when needs and

142

anxieties are daily becoming more urgent. The United Nations Development Program has an increasingly clearer grasp of its physical, intellectual and spiritual poverty, and the will to remedy it. If this is to be done, however, the whole world must become aware that poverty is not only an intolerable evil for its victim, but must also be so considered by every man worthy of the name. Man must indeed be enabled to survive, but he must also be given the means of living fully, as a person capable of founding a family and giving his children a satisfactory upbringing; these are the tasks that call for the disinterested help of all men of goodwill, surpassing all differences of nation, race, culture and religion. Moreover, the man of today ought to become more convinced of this as each day passes; it is his own existence that is at stake, and not optional assistance and emergency aid. All human resources must be mobilized, and it is not enough to give of one's possessions; one must give the best of oneself. The peace to which the world aspires will be built only at this price because, as has rightly been said, "development is the new name for peace."

These are the thoughts with which the forthcoming meeting at Milan inspires Us and which We thought it helpful to communicate to you, in Our desire to spare no effort to achieve, with the fruitful cooperation of all men of goodwill, peace in truth, justice, charity and freedom.

RESPONSE OF SECRETARY-GENERAL U THANT

I have had the greatest pleasure in conveying Your Holiness' inspiring words to Mr. Paul Hoffman, Administrator of the Program, and through him to the Governing Council. In doing so I have not failed to note again the clarity of vision and humanity of feeling with which Your Holiness recognizes and understands the problems of poverty and underdevelopment that beset the world and transcend all its political, racial and religious differences.

I share Your Holiness' view that, to be fully effective, the work of the United Nations in helping to resolve these problems must be carried out in the context of a universal awareness of the dangers which these problems hold for all mankind. Moreover, I remain profoundly conscious of the stimulus which Your Holiness has given and continues to give to the growth of that awareness.

I take the liberty of expressing to Your Holiness my warmest personal regards.

APPENDIX II

Address to the United Nations by
His Excellency Dr. Kenneth David Kaunda
President, Republic of Zambia

November 15, 1966

Mr. President,

About twenty-four months ago, I stood on this rostrum representing the youngest of the family of independent and free nations. At that time, Zambia's future was merely a hope overcast by doubt in certain minds among veterans of independence; indeed, it was a queer mixture of fear and hope among certain sections of our white community. However, for the majority of Zambians, the future was more than a hope, more than an expectation; it was something we cherished as we do today.

Two years of independence have more than fulfilled these hopes and have generated renewed confidence even among those who entertained fears about their future. The long

145

shadows of doubt have been replaced by rays of hope and greater faith in the bright future. I cannot, Mr. President, boast that Zambia is an oasis of undisturbed tranquility.

But the multi-dimensional forces unleashed by independence have opened the floodgates to development, before considered by the colonial administration as beyond the realm of practical possibility, in every conceivable field of human life, coupled with the freedom and liberty of all human beings to participate in economic, social and political life without let or hindrance. The masses, both rural and urban, are now able to contribute freely and are only limited in their operations to improve their lot not by any institutional impediments but by forces beyond their own individual control.

Independence, despite problems that come with it which are a familiar phenomenon of every state, has enabled us to obtain from each able citizen, regardless of race or colour, a fair supply of effort for organisation in the developmental process for the improvement of society as a whole. Maximum cooperation from the people, by whose authority we govern, has been an inspiration to my government in the execution of development plans. At no time since the dawn of Zambia's colonial history and experience have conditions displayed such dynamism and propitiousness for greater development of the economy and society; at no time has confidence in the future risen to such unprecedented heights. These, Mr. President, are in my opinion among the essential conditions that beget stability, peace and progress which are the greatest concern of this Organisation.

Mr. President, my government and people have not only been preoccupied with stability and progress for Zambia alone. We are conscious and mindful of our international obligations not only as a member of the United Nations, but as a participant in other international and regional organisations which functionally together form, in our view, a huge complex machinery for the preservation of stability, peace and security the world over, and for the promotion of genuine understanding, cooperation and progress in the international community. We have great faith in the United Nations Organisation as an instrument for the maintenance of international peace and security and we shall continue working within it to maximize our contribution to the welfare of mankind. Our choice of non-alignment as a basic attitude in our approach to relations and problems among nations enables us to work freely for our goals in our struggle to help strengthen peace and conditions for greater progress.

Zambia feels great concern at the failure of nations to resolve their differences in an atmosphere of friendship and understanding, nor are we satisfied with the progress being made in the field of control of the proliferation of nuclear weapons and general disarmament. Indeed how can we be satisfied with the present state of international relations when there are before us such outstanding and delicate problems as the war in Vietnam, apartheid in South Africa with its twin sisters, the Rhodesian rebellion and the South-West Africa question, with the allied problem of the liberation of Angola, Mozambique and Portuguese Guinea. There are the problems of Germany and Korea with the continuing Cold War and its consequences, and, of course, the controversy over the admission of the People's Republic of China to the United Nations, as well as events in Africa and the Middle East. All these are a source of international unsettlement, and have tended to limit the achievements of the United Nations in its practical operation. Even so, its efforts are to be commended, particularly in the field of economic cooperation for development in which its specialised agencies have created such a great and unprecedented impact in technological advancement for the developing countries. What is required of us as members is now not only greater understanding and cooperation, but a complete and unreserved commitment to principles and objectives as clearly defined and envisaged in the Charter of the United Nations. It is not enough to declare oneself committed to these principles, ideals and objectives; one must act and be seen to act in the spirit of the Charter, and in the interests of the Organisation. The narrower definition of "national interests" and the egocentrism of this generation, coupled with the protectionist outlook of member nations, have prevented the smooth running of the Organisation in the pursuit of its objective.

If we are, and I quote the preamble of the Charter of the United Nations, "to save the succeeding generations from the scourge of war, which twice in our lifetime has brought untold sorrow to mankind," if we are, and I quote again, "to establish conditions under which justice and respect for the obligations arising from treaties and other sources of international law can be maintained," and if we are to help promote social progress and better standards of life among all human beings in larger freedom not only in our lifetime but in the lives of generations yet unborn, then we must make a move to eliminate now the sources of friction, conflict or misunderstanding which are responsible for the present unsettlement in international relations and the threats to peace and security.

Mr. President, the need for genuine objective understanding, untainted by prejudice, is not tomorrow, but now. This is also the time when action must be taken if we are to improve the state of international relations and pave the way for greater stability for the security and progress of all mankind.

However, the war in Vietnam has been exercising the thinking of my government for a long time. We are gravely concerned over the loss of lives and property in this war. Vietnam is a political problem and a lasting solution can only be achieved by all parties concerned taking a full part in devising the ways and means of ending the war. Mr. President, the present state of the war does not, in our view, offer any prospects favourable for a permanent and happy settlement.

We believe that the return to the 1954 Geneva Accords is the most urgent step after the cessation of hostilities, as a basis for negotiation. As long as the Vietnam war continues, there can be no relaxation of tension in Southeast Asia and this will continue to be a source of weakness in the United Nations peace-keeping machinery.

As I indicated earlier, events in Africa ranging from general instability within particular states to coups and confrontations between states, are a source of grave concern for bridge builders in stability and international cooperation. They are to be deplored not only because of the consequences to Africa and its search for order and stability, but also because they rob the continent of its potential to contribute effectively to the peace and security of the world as a whole.

The convulsions on that continent only add to the many problems of this Organisation; they reduce the areas of agreement and add to areas of tension of which there are already more than enough to divert this Organisation from its more positive functions of promoting social and economic progress for all.

Though presumably disappointing, events in independent Africa are from one point of view only to be expected and can only be analysed and more correctly understood in their proper perspective of an on-going historical development. Independent Africa, after a period of severe restraint and exploitation by colonial administrations for the benefit of metropolitan countries, has now unleashed the dynamic forces of every description and dimension, which were not allowed to grow and flourish before independence.

The opening of the floodgates for the free and full interplay of domestic and foreign forces has brought with it greater and brighter expectations resulting in what is sometimes called the "revolution of rising expectations." To control and guide the chain of revolutions or rapid changes in political, social and economic life is Africa's challenge.

The process of readjustment cannot be expected to be short and always smooth and peaceful. Governments in Africa are confronted with the unenviable task of telescoping technological development, and by normal standards they are doing well. Indeed even at the pace at which industrialization took place in Europe, for example, there were political, economic and social problems of immense magnitude, at least for that era.

To think that Africa should have succeeded in telescoping technological advancement without the present apparent instability is to display a wrong expectation; it is to misread the history of human development. As long as technological advancement implies reorganization in methods of economic activity such as industrial, agricultural and other production processes with their impact on social and political life which accompany such transformation, readjustment must be expected.

The faster the rate at which governments move to enforce the transformation, the greater the disparity in the relationships between institutions which have hitherto perhaps formed the basic foundation of normal political, economic, social life of the electorate.

The movement for African unity is facing this problem squarely and there can be no illusions, and it is better realized than ignored. This is not the forum in which I should discuss African unity. I, however, must make this point: the stability of the world, its security and progress now and in future depend, *inter alia,* upon the degree and the nature of Africa's contribution.

The world needs Africa as much as Africa needs the rest of the world. We are one and all partners for stability, peace and progress. Stability in Africa can best be achieved by a common understanding of problems; progress and prosperity are a product of cooperation on the continent itself in the first instance.

It is in the interest of the international community to encourage the forces of African unity on the road to the relaxation of international tensions and enlarging the areas of agreement. The United Nations as a supranational body must have an interest in the movement for African unity as a source of strength in the maintenance of peace and security.

Mr. President, it is unrealistic to talk of African unity and peace and stability in that continent unless the major problem of race is resolved. Race and its twin sister, colour, threaten the peace and stability of Africa; the confrontation based on colour will be the major factor in international unsettlement in the rest of the twentieth century as ideology and the cold war have been in its first half.

The spectre of a racial conflict on a global scale and the consequences for the world cannot be but frightening to all peace-loving nations. Yet this is what Southern Africa, under white totalitarian minority regimes, presents in South Africa, South-West Africa and Rhodesia; in Angola and Mozambique where millions of Africans, peace-loving human beings at that, are still the subject of rule by force against their will, exercised by racialist minorities for their own ends but to the detriment of the majority.

The process of decolonization and democratization which has brought about the independence of hundreds of millions in Africa has now run into a full gale of racialism and economic self-interest in Africa south of the Zambezi.

What is the nature of the conflict in southern Africa? In a

nutshell, first, it is one of colour. A few thousand white immigrants found themselves in the midst of a rich black-inhabited country; different in culture, and feeling different from the indigenous race, they could not look elsewhere for the defence of their interests but within their socio-cultural group for strength—their would-be protective umbrella, the country of their origin not being practically within reach.

Hence, second, religious fanaticism based on certain misconceptions about the nature of man became a unifying force within the white community, a community of the chosen with a destiny which only the white are privileged to have!

An appeal to race superiority, to the concepts of master and slave, of the Christian and the heathen, to western civilisation and its undefined opposite—all these form rallying points in the maintenance of the status quo in that area; it is a source of unity which feeds the undercurrent of fear of competition from the majority for economic and political control if principles of democracy and the fundamental human rights were respected.

This is the third aspect of the conflict, it is the factor which has made the struggle brutish, severe, prolonged and complex. What began as a very severe form of discrimination, segregation and separation is now official apartheid which, through a variety of devices, has enabled the three million whites to bar by every possible means including brutal force the economic, social and political advancement of millions of people in South Africa.

Fear of competition from the majority—the fate of the poor white—was partly the main reason for the discrimination and apartheid, but since then, it has also turned into a ruthless struggle for survival of the white race; thus we find the architects of apartheid who are the motivational force behind its development edifying this dogma.

The result is a chain reaction of fear breeding fear, suspicion, prejudice, hatred, and then as the screw of apartheid is tightened, the inevitable explosion must occur. Through a blind obsession, the authorities have defied and perverted all moral, legal and scientific arguments to sanction white superiority; they will go to any extreme to maintain their special privileges and to deprive the nonwhite majority for all time, if they could, of their fundamental human rights.

Apartheid is thus a dangerous rationalization of an instrument protectionist in purpose, but defeatist in fact and destructive in the final result. This is the nature of the counterforce met by decolonisation to which we as members of the United Nations are committed by a General Assembly Resolution of 1960; this is the counterforce over which the United Nations must prevail if only to help reduce the area of tension and enlarge the areas of agreement and cooperation.

I would like to emphasize that the accelerating fanaticism of apartheid would not have made the successful but deadly strides which it has made in South Africa were it not for the overt and open support, the confidence which the white totalitarian regimes have received from certain Powers and their financiers who have poured investment capital in thousands of millions of pounds, as well as expanding their trade.

How many resolutions have been discussed in this Assembly, in the Security Council, in the Trusteeship Council, in our effort to correct the present course in South Africa's political, social and economic development? How many of those have failed to go through as a result of opposition, open or overt, by certain major powers?

Britain's attitude on Rhodesia, for example, can only be described as one of prohibitive procrastination in the interest of the minority. I repeat, Mr. President, it is not enough for those with cosmopolitan interests simply to declare their commitment to principles of democracy.

It is not enough for those possessing the power and the means to resolve situations and reduce world tensions simply to, and I quote the preamble of the United Nations Charter, "reaffirm faith in fundamental human rights, in the dignity and worth of the human person, in the equal rights of men and women of nations large and small"; major powers must be committed to principles both by verbal declarations and by deeds. There is need to demonstrate such commitment in practice.

Those in positions of leadership of this generation must exercise not only paramount but responsible authority over the affairs of their fellow men. Leadership to be worth exercising and asserting must be genuine, responsible and be in the interest of those over whom it is being exercised. Leadership without wider morality is brutal leadership and is not worthy of the human society.

Successful leadership does not only call for political ingenuity and clever manipulation of awkward situations, nor the scoring of diplomatic victories and the inflicting of defeats; it calls above all for the mastering of all moral stamina, courage, honesty and dedication to face the truth and to shape and steer the ship of humanity perpetually on its proper course to safety, stability and peace for the progress and happiness of all. Never before in history have these qualities of leadership been more in demand than today when the world is so delicately balanced between survival and destruction.

I call upon the Member Nations of the United Nations and implore the major powers most concerned to take the first practical steps in the right direction by sanctioning positive measures in the light of the known conditions, to remove now the dangerous source of a possible major racial conflict in southern Africa. To this end, Zambia has given its fullest and unqualified support to the resolution recently passed in this

General Assembly condemning South Africa's maladministration of South-West Africa calling for the termination of her mandate over that territory, and establishing a United Nations body to take over the responsibility for its future development and welfare.

Mr. President, may I, on behalf of my government and the people of Zambia, congratulate the General Assembly for this very important step. In particular, let me congratulate the major powers; the United States and the USSR for providing the necessary support for the resolution on South-West Africa —so vital, if implemented, to the future of Southern Africa and the peace of the world.

This achievement by the General Assembly is even the more welcome and heartening, coming as it does after the unfortunate judgement on this issue by the World Court. For our part, I wish to make this pledge: Zambia will continue to give its unqualified support to any measures or proposals aimed at bringing about an early end to the current unhappy state of affairs in South Africa and South-West Africa, to the conflict among races and men of colour. We pledge our support for measures calculated to bringing about a situation in which human rights will be respected and observed, in which there will be a permanent, lasting and just settlement in the interest of peace and harmony among races and progress and happiness for all.

Mr. President, the passage of the Resolution on South-West Africa is the highest demonstration so far in the international community of the universal condemnation of not only apartheid but the tyranny exercised by the few human beings over the majority, of our concern for peace, justice and the principles of the Charter of the United Nations Organization. We should, therefore, not only give nominal support to this resolution, but we must all *now* prepare for its early implementation

without delay. At this juncture let me earnestly implore those
of you who are members of the Security Council to ensure the
smooth and rapid passage of the Resolution when it comes
before you so that we can place the people of South-West
Africa firmly on the road to self-determination and independence, thereby enabling them to work their own destiny in
freedom, a God-given right.

The illegal declaration of independence by a few thousand
white people in order to enable them to impose their will on
the majority and against all known principles of law and human justice, and in order to preserve white privileges and
maintain domination, is an abomination sanctified. Britain,
for all her earlier declarations in condemnation of the illegal
acts, has shown remarkable resistance to take swift and effective measures to bring down the rebel regime and restore
constitutional rule.

Indeed, a few days back, the rebels celebrated their first
anniversary of illegal independence. To them the illegal and
undemocratic declaration of independence is an act of courage and a mark of victory. To the majority of the people in
that country the memory of what amounts to treachery by
Britain will be bitter. It is not only Smith who is guilty of
treacherous acts, but Britain, as an administering power, a
country that claims to have responsibility over the rebel colony, but at the same time refuses to discharge that responsibility.

Britain is by stages betraying the four million people in the
interest of the two hundred thousand whites. Indeed of late,
some British opposition leaders have been sincere in revealing
their concern for the fate of the people they refer to as of their
own stock, while those in government have openly admitted
to be sheltering Smith and his fellow rebels from Africa and
world opinion.

Mr. President, Britain's handling of the Rhodesian crisis

makes shameful reading; it is a painful experience for those of us who are genuinely interested in and committed to the cause of peace, stability and freedom through justice; for peace without justice, without the respect of human rights, is only an uneasy peace; it quickly leads to instability. It is not my intention to bore this Assembly with rhetoric over the inconsistencies, duplicity and contradictions in Britain's Rhodesia policy.

Nor do I need to dwell on the failure of the voluntary economic sanctions policy and the erroneous theories upon which it is based. I do not need to emphasize the dismal failure of sanctions. This everybody knows, including Britain.

But, Mr. President, I think it is important to point out that the attitude of prohibitive reluctance which Britain has displayed throughout the Rhodesian crisis is in itself a confirmation of her policy of an ultimate "honourable defeat" which cannot to us be but dishonourable and downright sell-out.

In pursuit of this policy, it is our conviction that Britain is seeking to disengage herself from the problem and ultimately wash her hands of it, leaving the fate of the four million at the mercy of a ruthless minority. The lesson of what happened in 1910 in South Africa and its aftermath is too recent to be ignored.

This could be disastrous not only to the people of Rhodesia but also to Africa and the United Nations, whose interests will be sacrificed just for the sake of appeasing the rebel regime and its mentor South Africa. I must emphasize that this policy which has allowed the rebels to build a series of steps towards a violent racial explosion makes the British government an accessory before and after the fact, and that government cannot escape the responsibility for the turbulent and tragic events which will follow. I call upon all members of the United Nations to prevent any attempt at a mass sell-out.

For our part in Zambia, we diagnosed the problem before

the illegal act was declared. I told the British government that only force would prevent an illegal Declaration of Independence. I advised Mr. Wilson to do the right thing at the right time. He did not do so. After the illegal Declaration of Independence, I again advised the British Premier to take short, swift and effective measures if he was committed to principles and to quelling the rebellion. He did not do so. Instead he chose a policy of voluntary sanctions.

My Government has urged the British government not only to recognize that the Rhodesian crisis is a moral issue, but to consider its consequences for Zambia's policy of non-racialism. Indeed, I have told the British government repeatedly and in no uncertain terms through every channel at my disposal that the continued existence of the rebellion, the basic aim of which is to perpetuate for all time, if possible, the inhuman oppression and exploitation of the four million by a bare two hundred thousand people, places our own way of life, in which race and colour of a man's skin do not count, in jeopardy.

We have not failed to impress upon the British government as a matter of principle that non-racialism at this hour in the breakdown of international barriers is a step further in the development of civilization; that we consider this as Zambia's, and indeed the rest of independent Africa's, greatest contribution to human development for which we are prepared to fight to the end. It is right, it is noble, it is just.

To date, the Common Services owned jointly by ourselves and Rhodesia like the Railways, the Kariba Hydro-Electric Scheme, the Central African Airways, which provide Zambia with her vital power supplies and her communications and external trade links and whose headquarters are all in Rhodesia and for all practical purposes controlled from Salisbury, cannot be properly operated and administered in the absence of a legal government in Rhodesia.

To date our economy is strained also as a result of the maximum cooperation in the economic sanctions if only to show Britain the futility of such measures in the Rhodesian crisis. We remain even more convinced that nothing short of force or mandatory sanctions under Chapter VII of the United Nations Charter, Articles 41 and 42, will bring about the conditions favourable for the normalization of the administration of Rhodesia. The illegal Declaration of Independence is an act of war on the four million people who are not consulted even in the current negotiations to end the rebellion.

Mr. President, it is sad, very sad indeed, to compare the slaughter at Sharpville in South Africa, the ruthless and inhuman laws, the indignities suffered by the black people of South Africa, the Rhodesian rebellion, the shooting of "whole gangs" of humanity and the detention of the thousands of Africans in Smith's concentration camps on the one hand, and the action taken when black rebels in what is now Kisangani held white people as hostages.

In Rhodesia a lunatic fringe have taken over the administration, more than four million people are held as hostages; the Smith regime can mete out any measures to Africans, detain, restrict, imprison with impunity. World reaction, particularly certain Western powers, shows little or no understanding. If they understand, then they show little or no inclination to take as positive a stand as that taken during the time of the incident in Kisangani in 1964. Are two hundred thousand white people better citizens of Rhodesia than the four million black people?

Are we to believe now that human rights are indivisible, except in Southern Africa; are we to accept that equality of human beings before law is true, but not in Southern Africa? Can we legitimately exclude the People's Republic of China from the international community but accept the minority governments in southern Africa? On what basis: moral, ethical, human, political?

Are we to continue supporting an economy based on repressive social and economic legislation and practice against the fundamental principles of human rights and justice which are entrenched in the United Nations Charter merely because we earn two hundred and fifty million pounds in trade each year and maintain thousands of millions of pounds in investment?

Equally striking is the fact that everywhere in independent and free Africa white minorities are enjoying their life without discrimination by the majority. I have yet to find an African country where white people are subject to indignities and other inhuman practices purely on the basis of colour.

Mr. President, just what kind of world are we building for ourselves and for posterity? We in Zambia are determined in our struggle to help build a decent world order, an edifice which human art can imagine neither grander nor fairer; we are determined to build it in such a way that it shall be fitting to a heart that has become wondrously great, uniting within itself the souls of all citizens fused into one whole. Hence our policy of non-racialism.

Mr. President, a decent world order is an academic exercise without international understanding and cooperation. Such a state of international relations is well nigh impossible of achievement in this age without resolving the problem of race. Peace, understanding and cooperation do not lie in chambers like this one, nor in covenants alone; they lie in the hearts and minds of all people, in every South African, Rhodesian, white and black, and in you and me.

Mr. President, those who are trying to bring about a semblance of peace in southern Africa by appeasing the white minorities, those who honour the Charter of the United Nations on human rights more in breach than in observance, are sowing seeds of destruction for the prospects of peaceful development of society, integrated and dynamic. Let it be remembered that while the two hundred thousand whites can make life difficult for the Africans, those four million Africans could rule out forever any prospects of racial harmony in Rhodesia.

Britain and her allies may be deluded into believing that there is peace in Rhodesia and southern Africa as a whole, but a peace that is maintained by force cannot be described as peace. It is not an imposed peace we seek, it is not peace maintained by police dogs, tear gas, saracens, guns and other instruments of oppression and coercion. This is not the peace that Zambia can work for; this is a perversion of peace to maintain white privilege and domination.

This is not the peace envisaged in the United Nations Charter, Mr. President. What we seek is genuine peace—not merely peace for a particular country, but peace for all men and women, for all mankind regardless of race or colour. We want genuine peace in our time, for all time and for generations to come.

If we desire peace and progress in South Africa, let us examine our own attitudes towards human rights and towards possibilities for peace now and for generations to come. The misfortune in South Africa is that men and women of goodwill have been driven to despair, thinking that the situation is impossible. I believe the problem of southern Africa is man-made and is not beyond the realm of human control. The world has got the capacity and the means to deal with the problem.

Mr. President, the United Nations is an organization for peace and security for all nations large and small, for all peoples, for the protection of their fundamental freedoms and human rights now and in the future. The peace-keeping machinery must be free from racial prejudice and must be totally committed to principles, ideals and goals of peace. Otherwise it cannot in all honesty meet its international obligations.

Since the eighteenth century when the first signs of the growth of nation states appeared, there has been a breakdown of international barriers, and technological advancement has made all of us more conscious of our belonging to one world, one human race with one common destiny. South Africa, South-West Africa, Rhodesia, Angola, Portuguese Guinea and Mozambique are pockets of resistance which must be overcome if we are to achieve our objective and if we are to honour our obligations under the Charter.

For those believers in freedom and Western-type democracy, I must emphasize that both these are on their death-bed in southern Africa, suffering from suffocation by the remorseless grip of apartheid and totalitarian rule. If, Mr. President, we have global interests and clashing commitments, these must be matched by responsibilities not only to our own citizens but also to the world and the future generations.

Mr. President, let us unite our strength not only to maintain international peace and security, but also to mobilize our resources for the promotion of economic and social advancement of all people. In order to achieve this, we must continue to work for genuine international understanding and co-operation and so creating conditions in which human rights and fundamental freedoms for all, without distinction as to race, sex, language or religion, will be respected and honoured, particularly in southern Africa.

In this way we should ensure the march of all nations with God, in freedom and harmony; in this way we should ensure a just and lasting peace on earth and goodwill towards men.

Thank you, Mr. President.

APPENDIX III

Address by Ousmane Soce Diop
Ambassador and Permanent Representative
of the Republic of Senegal to the United Nations
University of Carbondale, Illinois

October 21, 1965

I have the great honor of being invited by the University of Carbondale to speak to you of the Senegalese vision of the world of '65, and in particular of our conviction that improved communication among men is a fundamental condition for human progress and universal peace.

You all know that, following national independence, what our young nations of Africa need most is economic and social development in order to improve the living conditions of our masses. Political independence must not be an end in itself. It must merely be the means of giving our people better food, better housing, better health, and decent training and education for the rising generations. From the beginning, we have understood that to achieve all this, we would first have to build

163

and put into operation a complete network of all communication media: roads, telecommunication, radio, films, educational television, as well as lectures by rural extension agents and technical assistance experts. All of that for education because without it it is impossible to meet our most pressing needs in economic and social development. In this connection, universal primary instruction on all levels of the population, even to the most remote village in the bush (the basic social unit of the country), proves to be the indispensable tool without which no economic development or social progress is possible.

The task is immense. Imagine that one-third of Senegal's national budget is allocated to primary education alone and that, in spite of this great sacrifice, outside the large cities, in the rural areas where 90 percent of our population lives, we are able to offer such education to only one-third of the children.

Until our rural masses have all received the rudiments of primary education, it is certain that no means of communication—whether it be books, press, radio, cinema, educational television, or rural extension workers—will be able to reach all the layers of our population.

Once all our children are in school, our masses will be open to all communication media, and thus to all possibilities of achievement.

We have made the following observation: the execution of our development plan has been most effective along the tar-surface roads and the major bush tracks, because there the settlements have schools and more numerous and varied means of communication with the rest of the country—by newspaper, radio, travellers' reports, and the cinema.

However that may be, one thing is sure: without first educating the masses, no development will be possible. Indeed, through multilateral as well as bilateral assistance, machines, capital and experts have been made available to the people of the undeveloped world. But it must be said that the results which might have been expected from such aid have not been forthcoming. Often it has simply been forgotten that it is necessary to start with the individual, raising him up from his ignorance through education.

After this preparation, the rural masses would be able to understand fully the need for economic and social progress and wish to work toward it. Too, they could be trained to run the machines they are given, and to use them more effectively. Through education they would also be enabled to make wise use of money and other means of development. In short, with their own effort and the material put at their disposal by outside assistance, preparatory education would allow them to ensure their own economic and social development.

You see, therefore, the importance of communication as a factor in mass education. Through books, radio, movies and talks by rural agents employed as instruments of education and technical training, the people must be given the rudiments of the elementary knowledge necessary in order to put to good use all the material factors of progress. For example, through films, talks given by rural extension experts, popular science pamphlets, radio, or educational television programs, the masses can be taught to use fertilizers and selected seed effectively, how to can, or how to improve farming and stock-raising methods. It is obvious that man and his education are the basic elements of the economic and social progress of the developing world.

On the international level, the expansion of communication media is just as pressing a need as it is on the national level. As soon as possible, books, newspapers, cinema, educational television, lectures and cultural exchanges should be made available to all. In this way it will be possible to create and develop better understanding among continents, men, and their respective civilizations. We should without delay proceed to take an exhaustive inventory of the artistic and cultural stock of all peoples in order to conserve it so that it may become a part of the universal civilization. Before the end of this century this universal civilization should become the culture of all men on this planet.

We must become acquainted with all civilizations and all original cultures of all the races before they perish under the increasingly overwhelming pressure toward the international standardization of man.

For Africa's part, we have made a definitive choice to return to the original sources of our Negro-African civilizations in order to make our own contribution to the universal culture in which all human cultures must play a part. Our attitude on this matter has come to be called the "Negritude Movement."

This movement is, most certainly, a refusal on our part to withdraw from society. Soon after our national independence, President Senghor, speaking in Florence on what direction we would give to the evolution of our cultures, launched a slogan concerning the creation of a universal culture where we would go, not in an effort to mimic as perfectly as possible the canons and models of other civilizations no matter how illustrious they may be, but rather where we would take our own contribution based on the most authentic sources of our own civilizations.

When we reach this final great meeting point of all human cultures, we do not want to go as mere consumers, but instead as creators of civilization, thus paying our own quota to the universal heritage.

This attitude, moreover, intentionally or not, has been that of the Afro-Americans, I mean the Americans of African origin. Uprooted from Africa and transplanted onto a foreign soil where, through the centuries, they have even forgotten their ancestral tongues, they turned inward. Then, in the deepest inner meditation, they heard the reminiscing of their whole being, their whole soul. Instinctively, they created Negritude before the word was coined. They re-created the rhythms, songs and dances of Africa. They even reconstituted African philosophies and cosmogonies. Touching on this subject, I wrote the following not long ago, in a poem entitled "Tomango":

> Like the children of Israel
> Under the whips of the Pharaohs
> You have never forgotten
> The Land of the Ancestors.
> Despite centuries of estrangement
> The soul and tradition of Africa
> Spring suddenly
> From the rock of the merengue,
> From the triumphant pain
> Of the negro spiritual,
> From the heart-rending chants
> Of Ella Fitzgerald,
> From the multicolored fires of Armstrong's trumpet
> And from the white-hot tom-tom beat
> Of your bursting drums.

Naturally, we realize the dangers of the Negritude movement. Pushed to a narrow sectarianism, in the end it would only become racism in reverse. Our friends in other continents are already fearing this, and we are as aware of it as are they. That is why we have now put precise limits on this cultural movement. We, in dealing with this human problem, have adopted the attitude which has been so brilliantly defined by the Hindu poet, Rabindranath Tagore. He said, "I want the fresh wind of every culture and of every civilization to waft freely through my abode, but not so strongly that I am blown away myself."

Before concluding, it must be stressed that our visions of the world of '65 must converge toward a solution of that great crisis of our contemporary history, namely, the existing imbalance between a fantastic scientific progress which has enabled man to destroy his planet with the atomic bomb and soon to walk around on the moon, while the progress of our moral consciousness has been static if not in open retrogression. According to Bergson, "the overgrown body awaits an extra measure of soul, and materialism is in need of a mystique."

This "extra measure of soul" can only be brought to all peoples on every continent through an extension of our communication media so as to allow the whole range of human civilizations to communicate with each other, to get to know one another in order that a universal symbiosis, infinitely enriching to each and every people, may emerge. Is the beautiful white sunlight when refracted by a raindrop not made of thousands of rainbow-fires?

The mystique which the technical progress of today's world needs is first of all a revival of spiritual values, and then a mystique based on brotherhood, mutual assistance, and a more equitable distribution of the world's wealth for the sake of universal peace and above any national or individual egotism. We must remember that before the end of this century, the world's population will have doubled due to the magnitude of the present population explosion, and that the world of the year 2000 will be an extraordinary world in which one man out of every two will be an Asian, and where three-fourths of the non-Asians will be from underdeveloped countries. Thus, seven-eighths of the world population will be composed of men living in underfed countries, in ignorance, sickness and poverty. In contrast, there will be one-eighth of the human population living in the industrialized countries, highly developed, with 90 percent of the world's resources in their hands and a correspondingly high standard of living. That is the disturbing view of the world in the next quarter-century, a world off balance where, with every passing day, the rich get richer and the poor poorer and more numerous. The impasse and the danger are well known. They have been studied by competent experts who have weighed them to the nearest gram and measured them to the nearest millimeter, but despite the great alarm which was sounded in Geneva in the spring of 1964 during the United Nations Conference on Trade and Development, no positive step has yet been taken. One has the impression that our contemporary world is marching toward the final impasse, the apocalypse, impelled by the same Fate which struck the hero of an ancient Greek tragedy. He advanced step by step, closer and closer to death, fully aware of what he was doing but unable to stop himself. The chorus of spectators, as powerless as he, could only cry "alas" in sympathy.

If we wish to escape the final impasse and its apocalyptic consequences, we must bring it about that human communication and exchange, trade in particular, are no longer governed only by the law of profit, the law of the sea among fishes and the law of the jungle among wild beasts, but rather by the mystique of justice, mutual assistance, and universal peace for the general welfare of all mankind.

APPENDIX IV

Address by
Chief S. O. Adebo, Ambassador and Permanent Representative
of Nigeria to the United Nations
Fordham University

March 1, 1966

I wish to take this opportunity to say a few words on a subject which I am sure is of interest to all of us—harmony among men—for is it not an undeniable fact that most of the world's problems, today as in the past, are the result of the lack of such harmony? At one time it was Jew versus Gentile, at another Christian versus Moslem. Religion, instead of promoting harmony, was in fact the cause of conflict among men, and a lot of shameful acts were perpetrated by man against man in the name of the Cross or the Crescent. One still hears, from time to time, in certain countries, of people advocating so-called "holy wars," but in reality the concept is outmoded and it can be said that the days of the worst manifestations of religious fanaticism are over.

170

Other causes of disharmony among men, unfortunately, still exist, ideological differences for instance. But the one to which I wish to draw attention this afternoon, my dear friends, is the abominable plague of racism. I think that racism is the greatest danger in the world today. My African compatriots and I are not alone in this view. Our view is shared by people like Lord Caradon, the British Minister of State who is chief representative of his country today at the United Nations.

Contrary to the impression given by certain countries which adopt a holier-than-thou attitude in this matter, racism is not practiced in only a few countries in the world. Wherever black people live in the same community with the whites, especially where they form or begin to become a significant proportion of that community, they have been victims of discrimination. In some places, the discrimination has taken a quite callous and undisguised form. In others it is practiced in a disguised, subtle fashion.

Racism has been a feature of this world for as long as anyone can historically recall. Why has it only now become the greatest threat to world peace? It is because racism is manifestly unjust, because the people of colour will no longer tolerate it, and because the conscience of the world as a whole is not what it used to be.

In the Preamble to the United Nations Charter, the States Members declare their determination "to reaffirm faith in fundamental human rights, in the dignity and worth of the human person," and in Chapter I they go on to declare that one of the objectives of the Organization is "to achieve international co-operation . . . in promoting and encouraging respect for human rights and for fundamental freedoms for all without distinction as to race, sex, language or religion." These declarations did not constitute the first recognition of racism as an evil. They merely confirmed the opinion already held by countless people all over the world, and they made the extermination of that evil one of the purposes of the United Nations. It is no longer possible for sane human beings to advocate or justify racism.

The practice of racism now constitutes an offence, an offence against the principles of the United Nations Charter, an offence of which the appropriate organs of that Organization are entitled to take notice. That is why these provisions of the Charter constitute a sort of Magna Carta for the anti-racism movement.

When the United Nations Charter was signed in San Francisco some twenty years ago, only a handful of countries of predominantly coloured composition were members of the Organization. Today the position is altogether different. More than half the membership is now Afro-Asian, including 37 African countries. In 1945 most of these countries were still under white domination, and were in varying degrees victims of colour discrimination, even within their own territories. Until a few years before the end of the Second World War, there were so-called European hospitals in Nigeria to cater for British members of the Nigerian civil service and other European residents of the country, and so-called African hospitals, with far inferior facilities, to cater for the indigenous black population. Today, the whites and the blacks in Nigeria attend the same schools, live in the same hotels if they can afford the charges, and resort to the same hospitals if they are sick.

But the battle for fundamental human rights for the man of colour was not confined to Africa. It has also been fought, as we are all aware, with equal determination in the United States of America, which contains the greatest black population outside of Africa itself. To Africans who know what conditions were in their different countries around the turn of the century, to Afro-Americans who know what the conditions were in the United States of America at around the same time, the progress that has been made by coloured people both inside and outside Africa has been most spectacular.

And yet there is no room for complacency in regard to the future. It would be idle to pretend that the battle has been completely won. It has not, and a great deal requires still to be done, both in Africa and outside it. In Africa, we still have Ian Smith and his racist regime in Rhodesia, we still have Dr. Verwoerd and his pro-apartheid regime in South Africa, and we still have the so-called Portuguese territories in our continent where self-determination is still but a dream. By the same token, in spite of the considerable progress achieved in recent years by Afro-Americans in the United States of America, it is recognized that they have still a long way to go before they can be said to have achieved equality of status and opportunities with other ethnic groups in the American Union. But the people of colour are no longer prepared to tolerate racism. We shall continue the struggle until the last racist citadel has fallen.

The black revolution is not a danger to the white races of the world. It is a movement for the promotion of racial harmony. The great Albert John Luthuli of South Africa, winner of the Nobel Peace Prize, put the position as follows:

Africa's fight has never been and is not now a fight for conquest of land, but for the recognition and preservation of the rights of man and the establishment of a truly free world for a truly free people.

The black revolution is therefore a challenge to the conscience of members of the white race.

Fortunately, as I indicated before, the conscience of the world is not what it used to be. The black revolution is not being furthered only by Africans and persons of African descent. It enjoys the support of peoples of other racial groups whose conscience or whose religion enables them to overcome the prejudices of centuries.

As a Christian, I am glad that the Christian church is a participant in this crusade. In his address from which I already quoted, Nobel Peace Prize winner Luthuli referred to the work of Christian missions in Africa as a mitigating feature of the unhappy situation that prevailed for many decades all over the continent and still continues until today in his own country. He said that "men like Dr. David Livingstone, and Dr. John Philips and other illustrious men of God stood for social justice in the face of overwhelming odds."

There are people of course who take the view that the church ought to stand aside from movements of this kind, indeed from any interest in social or political reform. There have always been such people, as is shown by the following extract from a statement made in 1942 by the late Archbishop Temple, who was head of the Anglican Church in Britain at the time and who, because of his progressive stance on social issues, was nicknamed "the People's Archbishop":

It is assumed that the church exercises little (political) influence and ought to exercise none: it is further assumed that this assumption is self-evident and has always been made by reasonable men. As a matter of fact it is entirely modern and extremely questionable.

The assumption that the church should keep out of movements aimed at making this a better world is no longer simply questionable. It is, in my submission, now absolutely dead. Its fate has been sealed by the action of churches of all denominations everywhere in the last few years. In the Protestant field, the World Council of Churches has been most active in this regard, and so has been the National Council of Churches of the United States in regard to action within this country. But the most dramatic action of all has been the promulgation of "Pacem in Terris" by the late Pope John XXIII, and the carrying forward of his interest by his successor, Pope Paul VI. In "Pacem in Terris," the late Pontiff said:

May all peoples of the earth become as brothers.

In his address to the United Nations during his historic visit to that Organization last year, Pope Paul amplified his predecessor's statement as follows:

Your vocation is to make not just some, but all people brothers . . . Men cannot be brothers if they are not humble. No matter how justified it may appear, pride provokes tensions and struggles for prestige, colonialism and egoism. In a word, pride shatters brotherhood.

Africa believes in the brotherhood of man, and Africans are prepared to continue to labour to promote such brotherhood, in spite of the odds against them. May I, in this connection, recall the words of a great son of Africa, whom Fordham was pleased to honour with a doctorate award in 1961, His Excellency Léopold Sédar Senghor, President of the Republic of Senegal? He said as follows:

The contributions of Africa will be to bring into the evolution of the world an element of love and to produce men without prejudices and men who will give light wings to reason.

And he continued as follows:

We are now, all of us, of different features, colour, languages, customs, stirred and carried by the same movement of life. We are on our way towards the world of tomorrow, the world of the civilization of the universal.

The leaders of the black revolution in Africa believe in the promotion of racial harmony as the best means of promoting the peace of the world. In the United States, we have Afro-Americans of equal stature and similar convictions, people like Martin Luther King and Ralph Bunche (both of them Nobel Peace Prize winners), Roy Wilkins, James Farmer and Whitney Young. Africans are not aiming for an Africa from which whites are driven out or excluded but one in which all the citizens of each country possess equal rights of political participation. And, as Martin Luther King pointed out in one of his characteristically vigorous but wise pronouncements the other day at a luncheon party at the United Nations, the Afro-American civil rights movement in the United States is not seeking a world of special privilege for men of colour but one in which all people of any and all colours can live together in perfect harmony. Well, how is the challenge posed by African and Afro-American leaders being received by the other side?

Fordham can be said to provide the answer to that challenge. The promotion of harmony among men is one of the great traditions of your University, a tradition that produced one of the great minds of this century, Pierre Teilhard de Chardin, a Jesuit priest, whose thoughts and writings are being pursued and studied at a special institute of Fordham University. That great thinker, in his formidable anthropological studies, recognized the varied mixtures making up mankind and the rich heritage characterizing each race. He saw the rising tide of nationalism and the eventual restoration of sovereignty to the colonial people. He was a scientist who applied for humanistic purposes the methods and discoveries made available by technological advances. His sense of progress demanded a synthesis of the scientific and technological with a human and spiritual. For Teilhard de Chardin the world was entering a period of cultural cross-fertilization in which the person or nation uniting with other persons or nations would not lose, but actually enhance, his or its individuality. He and our own Senghor were dissimilar in their background, for the one was a scientist and the other a poet-philosopher. But they saw a vision of the same world, the world of the Universal.

I congratulate you, Sir, for continuing to maintain this

laudable tradition by making your 125th anniversary an occasion for underlining your interest in humanity, your belief in the brotherhood of man, your acceptance of the leadership in practical interest which was given by the late Pope John and is continued by the present Pontiff of your church. You are demonstrating yourselves to be effective instruments of the Society of Jesus, who have always been in the vanguard of progress within the Roman Catholic Church.

I said earlier that I thought racism to be the greatest danger in the world today. I make no apology for emphasizing the point, because so many people in the world do not appreciate the explosion that could result in the near future from world negligence in dealing with the remaining pockets of racism in Africa. This negligence contrasts very sharply with the resolute action that is being taken by the United States Government and people in disposing of their internal racial problem. One of the photographs that I treasure most in my archives is that showing the celebrated march from Selma to Montgomery of March 1965. Why is that photograph such a great treasure to me? It is the photograph of people marching in furtherance of the cause for fundamental human rights for the Negro. In the front line of the march were people of all classes and creeds, people of both white and black colours. And they were marching together, for a cause in which they all believed. The march was a most inspiring spectacle, therefore, from my point of view. If the world, particularly the major Western countries, could face up to the unfinished business in the field of racism in Africa in the way in which this photograph shows that the people of the United States are prepared to face up to their unfinished business of securing equality of status and opportunities for the Negro, then it will be possible to prevent the eruption of a racial war in Africa which could engulf the whole world.

APPENDIX V

Address by
Thomas Patrick Melady
Manhattan College

June 14, 1966

All of us here—living in a city that is in many ways the capital of the world—can look with a feeling of rejoicing on the position of the human family in our world.

We stand on the threshold of an era which has ended most of the barriers that have separated man from man. The barriers of time and distance have almost vanished. Formerly we were separated by great distances. Since the guns of World War II became silent we have seen the shrinking of distances. How marvelous it is that instead of being geographically separated we now can live as next-door neighbors to one another.

The same dynamic forces that are ending time and distance have also ended for the most part man's political domination

178

of man. You and I, in the past few years, have seen the Afro-Asian peoples who were long dominated by outside forces emerge as independent states. With the exception of southern Africa, the peoples of color have the natural dignity of ruling themselves. Thus a main cause of alienation, another barrier separating man from man has been almost completely eliminated.

A third barrier that has separated one brother in the universal family from his other brother is the rich-poor silhouette. Here mankind has only begun to realize how much remains to be done.

When man was separated from man by time and distance and when one part of the world politically dominated the rest of the world, unity was impossible. Furthermore, these separations prevented man from at least being aware of the seriously inequitable situation in the world. The white North Atlantic members of the world community were affluent and becoming richer and the non-white part of the world was still cursed by poverty, illiteracy and disease and becoming more afflicted by the unholy trio. The situation has not changed but the awareness of this gross gap in living standards has begun to stir both sides of the inequality.

When we contemplate the implication that the majority of the world's non-white peoples who are now politically free have awakened with a determination to obtain a decent standard of living we can indeed rejoice.

Yes, we know that some fear what is called the rising expectations of the world's poor. Instead of facing these changes with joy they prefer to talk about the decadence of modern civilization or even the approaching end of the world. And, of course, there are the cynics and the negative critics—those who can never build but only destroy.

It should be clear to us that this defeatism is unhealthy and impotent. Once it overtakes us, all potential to build is destroyed.

Yet we must face the challenge of world poverty openly and courageously. These are the facts: the per capita income in North America is $2,200 with an average life span of 68 years. In black Africa the per capita income is less than $100 with a life span of around 40 years. In Asia the per capita income is around $106 with a life span of fifty-one years. The developed nations and the United Nations have all launched programs to help correct this inequity. But these programs have really only helped to enlighten the world about world poverty and misery.

We dare not rely only on our governments to do something about this. We now all live in the same city and the miserable of the world are our next-door neighbors. Nothing of significance has been done to end the growing gap between the rich and the poor—made more horrible because it is the white and non-white. This is your responsibility and mine. The rising determination of the Afro-Asian peoples to end their life of misery must now be matched by our determination. Together we can push forward and thus end another serious source of alienation.

This opportunity clearly points out our destiny: to participate with enthusiasm in the forward movement of mankind. Our enthusiasm is justified, as we have seen in our lifetime significant progress of mankind toward greater unity.

These vital forces for change have resulted in mankind becoming the ascending arrow. Our duty is to build the earth, to advance forward.

Teilhard de Chardin, the great philosopher who lived among us here in New York until eleven years ago, said "it is not the fear of perishing but the ambition to live" which throws man into this forward movement. Let us therefore do what is our destiny: the embracing of a conquering passion to sweep away the defeatism, the pessimism, the elements that still separate man, that still alienate man.

What method shall we follow? Here we can learn much from Vatican Council II.

Rooted in the stabilizing forces of God's presence, we should in our thinking on the problems of the world maintain an openness to all members of the universal family. This is no longer an age to rely on set formulas. Principles of life remain but programs of action must change.

This will require us to experiment in method. This may sometimes cause a little uneasiness and all experiments may not work.

But we must branch out quickly into all areas of human endeavor. The ascending arrow is moving so rapidly that we no longer have time for years of talk and planning, as we must effect changes now. Some of the crucial areas that require our immediate attention are:

1. Urban life.
2. Problems of automation.
3. The insidious depersonalization of mankind caused by dealing with masses and large numbers.

There are two institutions whose recent emergence into worldwide leadership gives us cause for enthusiasm as we face tomorrow.

The resurgence given to Christendom by Vatican Council II and being given personal direction now by Pope Paul VI has rendered new power and strength to the Church. The treasure house of truth has been opened to the world and is uplifting mankind in a single tide toward his Creator.

Now we are all living in the same city—mankind has created his own institution—the United Nations. This represents a new spirit to unify the vital human forces to push mankind forward. We all recall the 4th day of October 1965, when Pope Paul VI visited the United Nations. He said then "we might call our message a ratification of this lofty institution . . . The peoples of the earth turn to the United Nations as the last hope of concord and peace."

In the last few years, there has been a tendency by some to criticize the effectiveness of a world body such as the United Nations. Some have attempted to cast a doubtful shadow on the ability of an assembly composed of nations so vastly different in ideology, wealth, culture and size. As expected, there will be many difficult moments, some failings, countless hours of exhausting discussion, yet this great experiment requires endless energy and dedication to translate more fully an ideal into reality. It is an experiment which must not fail. Mankind has significantly benefited from the currents moving forward and the United Nations is one of these currents.

The Church and the secular society have generated a rapid movement which is taking mankind forward to a new sunrise.

Our destiny is to embrace those forward movements and to assist them in approaching even more rapidly the noble goals given to us.

In our enthusiasm for these developments we cannot overlook the one great cloud on the horizon—racism, the hatred brought about when man denies that another man, because of the accident of his color, was created by God as his brother.

We must strike out and destroy the ugly sin of racism as it will eliminate all possibility of harmony in the human family. Every dream that we have spoken of will fade away if corrective action against this ugly doctrine is not taken soon. What can we do? Much has been said about the role of government. Let us discuss here the role of private institutions.

We must exert every effort to generate a favorable climate

for men of all races to live as brothers. The need is so urgent and substantive aspects so vital that our private institutions must utilize every power at their command to enhance the dignity of the human family.

In this regard and because of the seriousness of the situation, we think especially of the various Christian churches. A good number of them—Catholic, Orthodox, Episcopalian and others, discourage their faithful from committing major infractions against the laws of God by refusing Communion to them until they have been freed from the immediate guilt of these sins by confessing them, promising amendment and doing penance.

In other words, in other areas of human behavior, these churches preach the positive aspects of the good life but warn their faithful that should they murder, commit adultery or steal, they have seriously offended God and must reconcile themselves with God before they can approach the Communion table.

It is, on the other hand, a known scandal that no such publicity is given to the grievous sins of racism. We fully understand why sins of racism are so serious. God made us all brothers in His likeness but the racist sets himself above God and denies this. Furthermore, the racist sins against the greatest commandment of them all—charity.

The racist commits these sins and sets himself above God when he refuses to sell his house, rent an apartment, when he refuses admission to his club or to give a job to his brother because of his color.

Certain Christian churches have found it effective to reinforce teaching on serious matters with a system of censure against serious transgressions of these teachings.

But when it comes to the grievous sins of racism where the sinner blasphemes God the Creator by denying that all men are created in His likeness, there is a reluctance to acknowledge this sin. As a result of this some non-white Christians are beginning to question the integrity of these institutions. And the Christian churches risk repudiation by the peoples of color unless these horrible sins that directly affect them are treated like other mortal offenses against God's dignity.

Racism is a serious sin and must be declared so and treated by the churches as they treat other serious offenses.

Activity on all fronts to eliminate the barriers and traditions that separate man from man is part of the mighty movement forward. An invitation has been extended to us: to embrace with passion the ascending arrow, to reject with equal passion the ugly offenses that separate man from man.

BOOKS, MONOGRAPHS AND ARTICLES RECOMMENDED FOR ADDITIONAL READING

CHAPTER ONE

RISE TO POWER OF THE AFRO-ASIAN PEOPLES

AL-RAZZAZ, MUNIF. *The Evolution of the Meaning of Nationalism.* Garden City, New York: Doubleday, 1963.

BERGER, MORROE. *The Arab World Today.* New York: Doubleday Anchor Books, 1964.

CRANE, ROBERT I. "India," *Asia in the Modern World,* HELEN G. MATTHEW, ed. New York: Mentor Books, 1963.

GHEDDO, P. *Le Réveil des Peuples de Couleur.* Paris: Les Editions du Centurion, 1957.

MELADY, THOMAS PATRICK. *The Revolution of Color.* New York: Hawthorn Books, 1966.

NEHRU, JAWAHARLAL. *Toward Freedom.* New York: John Day, 1941.

SCHRAMM, WILBUR. *Mass Media and National Development.* Stanford: Stanford University Press, 1964.

SIGMUND, PAUL E. (ed.). *The Ideologies of the Developing Nations.* New York: Frederick A. Praeger, 1962.

TAGORE, RABINDRANATH. *Nationalism.* New York: The Macmillan Company, 1917.

TOYNBEE, ARNOLD J. "Africa: Birth of a Continent," *Saturday Review,* December 5, 1964.
WERTHEIM, W. F. *Indonesian Society in Transition: A Study in Social Change.* The Hague: W. Van Hoeve, 1956.

CHAPTER TWO

WORLD POWER TODAY

ARMSTRONG, HAMILTON F. "A Close View of the Nonaligned," *The New York Times Magazine.*
CANTRIL, HADLEY. *The Pattern of Human Concerns.* New Brunswick, N.J.: Rutgers University Press, 1965.
DEUTSCH, KARL W., and FOLTSZ, WILLIAM J. (eds.). *Nation Building.* New York: Atherton Press, 1963.
LONDON, KURT (ed.). *New Nations in a Divided World.* New York: Frederick A. Praeger, 1963.
MARTIN, LAURENCE W. (ed.). *Neutralism and Nonalignment: The New States in World Affairs.* New York: Frederick A. Praeger, 1962.
MEAD, MARGARET. "The Underdeveloped and the Overdeveloped," *Foreign Affairs,* October, 1962.
Nonalignment in Foreign Affairs. Annals of the American Academy of Political and Social Science, vol. 362, November, 1965.
NORTHROP, F. S. C. *The Meeting of East and West.* New York: The Macmillan Company, 1960.
O'BRIEN, C. C. "Non-Alignment," *New Statesman,* April 8, 1966.
"Passions and Perils of Nationhood," in *Time,* March 11, 1966.
SETON-WATSON, HUGH. *Neither War Nor Peace.* New York: Frederick A. Praeger, 1960.

CHAPTER THREE

HISTORICAL DEVELOPMENT OF WESTERN POLICY

DIA, MAMADOU. *African Nations and World Solidarity.* New York: Frederick A. Praeger, 1961.
EASTON, S. *The Twilight of European Colonialism.* New York: Holt, Rinehart and Winston, 1960.
EISENBERG, PABLO. "Western Reactions to Pan-Africanism," in *The Philosophy of Pan-Africanism,* S. Okechukwu Mezu, ed. Washington, D.C.: Georgetown University Press, 1965, pp. 87–95.

EMERSON, RUPERT. *From Empire to Nation.* Cambridge, Mass.: Harvard University Press, 1962.

GRUNDY, K. W. "African Explanations of Underdevelopment: The Theoretical Basis for Political Action," *Review of Politics,* January, 1966.

KAUTSKY, JOHN H. (ed.). *Political Change in Underdeveloped Countries.* New York: John Wiley & Sons, 1962.

LEWIS, WILLIAM H. *Emerging Africa.* Washington, D.C.: Public Affairs Press, 1963.

McKAY, VERNON. *Africa in World Politics.* New York: Harper & Row, 1963.

MATTHEW, HELEN G. (ed.). *Asia in the Modern World.* New York: New American Library, 1963.

SHILS, EDWARD. *Political Developments in the New States.* The Hague: Mouton and Co., 1962.

SUFRIN, S. C. "Benevolent Neo-Imperialism," *Ethics,* October, 1965.

TWITCHETT, KENNETH J. "Colonialism: An Attempt at Understanding Imperial, Colonial and Neo-Colonial Relationships," *Political Studies,* XIII (October, 1965).

VARG, P. A. "Imperialism and the American Orientation Toward World Affairs," *Antioch Review,* Spring 1966.

ZARTMAN, I. WILLIAM. *International Relations in the New Africa.* Englewood Cliffs, N.J.: Prentice-Hall, 1966.

CHAPTER FOUR

VITAL ELEMENTS OF THE
AFRO-ASIAN POLITICAL COMPLEX

"African Socialism." Selected articles in *African Forum,* Winter, 1966.

ALMOND, GABRIEL A., and COLEMAN, JAMES S. *The Politics of the Developing Areas.* Princeton, N.J.: Princeton University Press, 1966.

ALROY, G. C. "Insurgency in the Countryside of Underdeveloped Societies." *Antioch Review,* Summer, 1966.

APTER, DAVID E. (ed.). *Ideology and Discontent.* New York: The Free Press of Glencoe, 1964.

BELL, DANIEL. *The End of Ideology.* New York: Collier Books, 1961.

BENHAM, FREDERIC. *Economic Aid to Underdeveloped Countries.* London: Oxford University Press, 1962.

CROZIER, BRIAN. *The Struggle for the Third World.* Chester Springs, Penn.: Dufour Editions, 1966.

DEAN, VERA MICHELES. *Builders of Emerging Nations.* New York: Holt, Rinehart and Winston, 1961.

Human Problems of Economic Development. Texts of lectures and summaries of discussions at the Pax Romana Assembly, Bombay, December 8–15, 1964. Bombay: Newman Association of India, 1965.

JESUS, CAROLINA MARIA DE. *Child of the Dark.* Translated from the Portuguese by DAVID ST. CLAIR. New York: E. P. Dutton, 1962.

KAREFA-SMART, JOHN (ed.). *Africa: Progress Through Cooperation.* New York: Dodd, Mead & Company, 1966.

LAFARGE, JOHN, S. J. *The Catholic Viewpoint on Race Relations.* Garden City, N.J.: Hanover House, 1956.

MCCORMACK, ARTHUR (ed.). *Christian Responsibility and World Poverty.* London: Burns & Oates, 1963.

MELADY, THOMAS PATRICK. "The Impact of Africa on Recent Developments in the Roman Catholic Church," *Race,* VII, 2 (1965), 147–55.

————, and BADUM, MARGARET. "Teilhard de Chardin and the Afro-Asian World," *Catholic World,* November, 1965.

MOSMANS, GUY. *L'Eglise à l'Heure de l'Afrique.* Belgium: Les Etablissements Casterman, 1961.

New York Times, January 9, 1966, p. 1.

Problèmes Africains (text and documents). March 10, 1966, pp. 1–12.

RIVKIN, ARNOLD. "Israel and the Afro-Asian World," *Foreign Affairs,* April, 1959.

VILAIN, PIERRE. "Vatican II Annonce le Concile du Tiers Monde," *Croissance des Jeunes Nations.* February, 1966.

VILLAIN, MAURICE. *S.M., Rythmes du Monde.* Saint André lez Bruges, XIII, 4 (1965).

CHAPTER FIVE

THE THIRD FORCE AND THE SINO-SOVIET WORLD

BRZEZINSKI, ZBIGNIEW (ed.). *Africa and the Communist World.* Stanford: Stanford University Press, 1963.

HYDE, DOUGLAS. *Communism in Asia.* London: Hinsley House.

KOLARZ, WALTER. *Religion and Communism in Africa.* London: Sword of the Spirit, 1962.
LEVI, W. "China's Asian Policy," *Current History,* September, 1966.
MIRSKY, G., and STEPANOV, L. *Asia and Africa: A New Era.* Moscow: Foreign Languages Publishing House, n.d.
MOSELEY, P. E. "Communist Policy and the Third World," *Review of Politics,* April, 1966.
NIKHAMIN, V. "The Soviet Union and the Developing Countries," *International Affairs* (Moscow), April, 1966.
Orbis (periodical), special edition, Winter, 1966.
RA'ANAN, U. "Moscow and the Third World," *Problems of Communism,* January, 1965.
RAY, H. "Policy of Russia Towards the Sino-Indian Conflict," *Political Quarterly,* January, 1965.
SCALAPINO, ROBERT A. (ed.). *The Communist Revolution in Asia: Tactics, Goals and Achievements.* Englewood Cliffs, N.J.: Prentice-Hall, 1965.
SCHAPIRO, L. "Soviet Dream of Africa," *Encounter,* February, 1965.
SCHATTEN, FRITZ. *Communism in Africa.* New York: Frederick A. Praeger, 1966.
SYLVESTER, A. "Cuban Lessons for the Developing World: Recent Impressions of a Visitor," *Contemporary Review,* February, 1966.
THORNTON, THOMAS PERRY (ed.). *The Third World in Soviet Perspective.* Princeton, N.J.: Princeton University Press, 1964.
WHEELER, G. "Soviet and Chinese Policies in the Middle East," *World Today,* September, 1966.

CHAPTER SIX

PRESENT POLICY OF THE UNITED STATES TOWARD THE AFRO-ASIAN WORLD

"America as a Pacific Nation: Symposium," *Saturday Review.* October 8, 1966.
"America's Permanent Stake in Asia," *Time* magazine, September 23, 1966.
CRABB, CECIL V. "The United States and the Neutralists: A Decade in Perspective," *Annals,* vol. 362, November, 1965.
HAVILAND, H. FIELD. "The United States and the United Nations," *International Organization,* XIX (Summer, 1965).

LEFEVER, ERNEST W. *Ethics and United States Foreign Policy.* Cleveland: World Publishing Company, 1957.

LOGAN, RAYFORD W. "An Assessment of Current American Influence in Africa," *Annals,* Vol. 366, July, 1966, pp. 99–107.

MOORE, B. "American Nightmare: Why We Fear Peasants in Revolt," *The Nation,* September 26, 1966.

NIELSEN, WALDEMAR A. *African Battleline: American Policy Choices in Southern Africa.* New York: Harper & Row, 1965.

ROSSI, MARIO. *The Third World.* New York: Funk & Wagnalls, 1963.

RESTON, JAMES. "The Press, the President and Foreign Policy," *Foreign Affairs,* July, 1966.

ROUCEK, J. S. "Pacific in Geopolitics," *Contemporary Review,* February, 1965.

SULZBERGER, C. L. *Unfinished Revolution: America and the Third World.* New York: Atheneum, 1965.

"United States Aid in Asia: Symposium," *Current History,* IL, 291 (November, 1965), 257–308.

WILCOX, WAYNE A. "Contemporary American Influence in South and Southeast Asia," *Annals,* vol. 366 (July, 1966), 108–116.

CHAPTER SEVEN

WESTERN EUROPE AND THE AFRO-ASIAN WORLD

DURDIN, TILLMAN. *Southeast Asia.* New York: Atheneum, 1966.

HANHAM, H. J. "Future of Africa." *African Affairs.* April, 1966.

MCNEIL, WILLIAM H. *The Rise of the West.* Chicago: University of Chicago Press, 1963.

"Our Turn Now (Tide Is Running the West's Way in Asia and Africa)," *The Economist,* March 19, 1966.

PANIKKAR, K. M. *The Afro-Asian States and Their Problems.* London: Allen & Unwin, 1959.

POPLAI, S. L. (ed.). *Asia and Africa in the Modern World.* Bombay: Asia Publishing House, 1955.

RIVKIN, ARNOLD. *The African Presence in World Affairs.* New York: The Free Press of Glencoe, 1963.

SCHWARTZ, HARRY. *China.* New York: Atheneum, 1965.

SOPER, T. "Independent Africa and Its Links with Europe," *African Affairs,* January, 1965.

WALZ, JAY. *The Middle East.* New York: Atheneum, 1965.

CHAPTER EIGHT

THE HOLY SEE AND
ISRAEL AND THE THIRD FORCE

Christian Intellectuals in Developing Society. Kandy, Ceylon: Publishers of Logos, 1965.

Comments by Alioune Diop, Director of Présence Africaine, in *Le Monde,* October 3–4, 1965.

CONGAR, YVES M. J., O. P. "The Catholic Church and the Race Question," *The Race Question in Modern Thought.* Paris: UNESCO, 1961.

DEAN, VERA MICHELES. *The Nature of the Non-Western World.* New York: New American Library, 1963.

DESAI, A. R. *Social Background of Indian Nationalism.* Bombay: Bombay University Press, 1948.

ELLIOTT, WILLIAM Y. (ed.). *Education and Training in the Developing Countries.* New York: Frederick A. Praeger, 1966.

FANON, FRANTZ. *The Wretched of the Earth.* New York: Grove Press, 1963.

GRAHAM, ROBERT A. *Vatican Diplomacy.* Princeton, N.J.: Princeton University Press, 1959.

JOBLIN, J. "Church in the World: A Contribution to Pluralism," *International Labor Review,* May, 1966.

KAPLAN, MORTON A. (ed.). *The Revolution in World Politics.* New York: John Wiley & Sons, 1962.

KERSTIENS, THOM. *The New Elite in Asia and Africa: A Comparative Study of Indonesia and Ghana.* New York: Frederick A. Praeger, Inc., 1966.

KREININ, MORDECHAI E. *Israel and Africa: A Study in Technical Cooperation.* New York: Frederick A. Praeger, 1964.

LACOUTURE, J., and BAUMIER, J. *Le Poids du Tiers Monde.* Paris: B. Arthaud, 1962.

LEBRET, L. J. *The Last Revolution.* New York: Sheed and Ward, 1965.

LEVI-STRAUSS, CLAUDE. "Race and History," *The Race Question in Modern Thought.* Paris: UNESCO, 1961.

LORCH, NETANEL. "Israel and Africa," *World Today,* XIX, 8 (August, 1963).

MACDONALD, ROBERT W. *The League of Arab States.* Princeton, N.J.: Princeton University Press, 1965.

MARTIN, LAURENCE W. (ed.). *Neutralism and Non-Alignment.* New York: Frederick A. Praeger, 1962.

"New Nations: The Problem of Political Development," *Annals of the American Academy of Political and Social Science,* March, 1965.

ROSTOW, W. W. *Economic Growth—A Non-Communist Manifesto.* Cambridge: Cambridge University Press, 1960.

SENGHOR, LÉOPOLD SÉDAR. *African Socialism.* New York: American Society of African Culture, 1959.

SILVERT, K. H. (ed.). *Expectant Peoples: Nationalism and Development.* New York: Random House, 1963.

STALEY, EUGENE. *The Future of Underdeveloped Countries: Political Implications of Economic Development.* New York: Frederick A. Praeger, 1961.

WARD, BARBARA. *Nationalism and Ideology.* New York: W. W. Norton, 1966.

CHAPTER NINE

THE UNITED NATIONS AND THE THIRD WORLD

BABAA, KHALID D. "The 'Third Force' and the United Nations," *Annals* of the American Academy of Political and Social Science, vol. 362 (November, 1965).

DAVIDSON, NICOL. "Toward a World Order: An African Viewpoint." *Daedalus,* vol. 95 (Spring, 1966).

ELLIS, W. W., and SALZBERG, J. "Africa and the United Nations: A Statistical Note," *American Behavioral Science,* April, 1965.

EMERSON, RUPERT. "Colonialism, Political Development and the United Nations," *International Organization,* XIX (Summer, 1965).

HOVET, THOMAS, JR. *Africa in the United Nations.* Evanston, Ill.: Northwestern University Press, 1963.

JOYCE, J. A. "Development Decade at Mid-Point," *Contemporary Review,* June, 1966.

KAREFA-SMART, JOHN. "Africa and the United Nations," *International Organization,* XIX (Summer, 1965).

LALL, ARTHUR. "The Asian Nations and the United Nations," *International Organization.* XIX (Summer, 1965).

MCWHINNEY, E. "New Countries and the International Law: The United Nations' Special Conference on Friendly Relations and Cooperation Among States," *American Journal of International Law,* January, 1966.

"Notes and Comment: Small Countries Now Independent and Eligible for Membership," *New Yorker*. June 25, 1966.

WARD, BARBARA. "The United Nations and the Decade of Developments," *World Justice,* VII (March, 1966).

WILCOX, FRANCIS. *The United Nations and the Non-Aligned Nations.* New York: Foreign Policy Association, 1962.

CHAPTER TEN

A NEW POLICY FOR THE WEST TOWARD THE AFRO-ASIAN WORLD

DUIGNAN, P., and GANN, L. "Different View of United States Policy in Africa." *Western Political Science Quarterly,* XIII (December, 1960), 918–23.

MAIR, LUCY P. *New Nations.* Chicago: University of Chicago Press, 1963.

ROSTOW, W. W. "Role of emerging nations in World Politics" (Department of State Bulletin), April 5, 1965.

TEILHARD, DE CHARDIN. *Building the Earth.* Wilkes-Barre, Penn.: Dimension Books, 1965.

UNITED STATES SENATE, Committee on Foreign Relations. 86th Congress, First Session. *United States Foreign Policy,* No. 4, Washington, D.C., 1959.

ZARTMAN, I. W. "Problems in American Policy Toward Africa," *Motive,* XXVI (January, 1966), 48–50.

INDEX

Adebo, S. O., 170–77
Afghanistan, 124, 127–28, 132
African Review, 61
Afro-Asian Conference (Cairo,
  1962), 23
Afro-Asian Journalists
  Association (AAJA), 68
Afro-Asian People's Solidarity
  Organization, 70
Agriculture, 51–52, 54, 62, 117
Ahidjo, Ahmadou, 69
Aiken, Frank, 104
Algeria, 13, 24, 62, 65, 124, 127
All-African Journalist Union, 62–63
All-African Trade Union Federation
  (AATUF), 63
Angola, 147, 151, 162
  Portuguese rule of, 40, 77, 95–97
Apartheid, 61, 78–83, 92–93, 147,
  151–62, 173
Aswan High Dam, 62

Belgium, 38, 82, 87–88, 94
  colonial policy of, 40
Ben Bella, Ahmed, 65
Berlin Conference (1884–85), 38
Boxer Rebellion (1900), 37–38
Bourguiba, Habib, 106
Burma, 15, 124, 126–27
Burundi, 24, 68, 124, 126

Cambodia, 124–28
Cameroons, 38, 62, 94, 99–101, 107,
  124, 127–28
  revolution in, 68–69
Canada, 20, 33
Caribbean states, 16, 122, 124, 126,
  128
Cassini Convention, 37
Catholic Church, 16–17, 109–15,
  120, 130, 177, 181–83. *See also*
  John XXIII; Paul VI
Central African Republic, 16, 124,
  127–28
China, 31, 35, 54, 75–76, 95, 132,
  136–37

French policy toward, 20, 90–91
  policies of, tested in Africa, 58,
    61, 65–70
  racism of, 23, 66, 68
  Soviet relations with, 13, 20, 23,
    36–38, 65, 70
  trade history of, 36–38
  UN and, 69, 124, 126–27, 147,
    159
Clark, Kenneth B., 85
Communism, 12–13, 20–28, 46, 101,
  132, 136. *See also* China; So-
  viet Union
  Afro-Asian view of, 22–23
  Chinese conversion to, 38
  influence of, on UN voting, 126–
    27
  outlawed in Africa, 64
  policies of, tested in Africa, 58–70
  as socialism, 54
  U.S. anti-Communism, 73–74
Congo, 24, 64–65, 68, 82, 94, 101
  Belgian rule of, 40
  UN and, 21, 104, 124, 126–28
Court of International Justice, 80,
  155
Cowan, L. Gray, 51–52
Culture, 51, 95–96, 108, 166–67
  Hispanic, 99–100, 103
  modernization balanced with, 52–
    53, 56–57
  superior, 34–35
  village mentality in, 48–49

Dallin, Alexander, 65
De Gaulle, Charles, 20, 90–91
Democracy, 49, 53, 162
*Diary of Carolina Maria de Jesus,
  The,* 42–43
Diop, Ousmane Soce, 47, 163–69
Diori, Hamani, 69–70
Disease, 16, 20, 110–11
Disraeli, Benjamin, 14
Dulles, John Foster, 74

East Africa, 16, 65
Egypt, 15, 66–67, 125

195

THE AUTHOR
AND HIS BOOK

DR. THOMAS PATRICK MELADY has been an observer of the third world since his first job in Ethiopia in 1955. An author, professor, foundation executive and lecturer, he is a leading authority on the Afro-Asian peoples, the peoples of color in all parts of the world and the problems of racial harmony.

His other books include *Profiles of African Leaders, White Man's Future in Black Africa, Faces of Africa, Kenneth D. Kaunda of Zambia,* and *The Revolution of Color.* Dr. Melady is a "doer" as well as a theorist and plays a leading role in organizations active in world affairs, race relations and ecumenical understanding.

The author was born in Norwich, Connecticut, where he received his elementary and high school education. He holds a B.A. degree from Duquesne University and M.A. and Ph.D. degrees from the Catholic University of America. He has also received five honorary doctorates and four governmental decorations.

Dr. Melady resides with his wife, the former Margaret Judith Badum, and daughter in New York City.

WESTERN POLICY AND THE THIRD WORLD was set in type by American Book–Stratford Press, Inc., of New York. The type face is Times Roman.

A HAWTHORN BOOK